AS THEY LIKE IT!

AS THEY LIKE IT!

A collection of recipes from the theatre

PRYOR PUBLICATIONS
WHITSTABLE, WALSALL

1997 PRYOR PUBLICATIONS
75 Dargate Road, Yorkletts, Whitstable,
Kent CT5 3AE, England
Tel & Fax (01227) 274655
Specialists in Facsimile Reproductions

Published by Pryor Publications
for
THE SOPHIE WINTER MEMORIAL TRUST ©

Regd. Charity No 1054146

Compiled by Margaret Maughan
Illustrated by Katherine Spring
Cover Design by Ted and Lyn Rockley
(from an idea by Camilla)

A CIP Record for this book is available from the British Library
ISBN 0 946 014 63 9

Typeset by Jilly Dolphin in Garamond

Printed and Bound by
Whitstable Litho Printers Ltd
Whitstable, Kent

Sophie Winter was my niece and when the Sophie Winter Memorial Trust was set up I wondered how I could help to raise funds. The idea came to me of compiling a cookery book made up of recipes from people connected with the theatre. I thought this would be a first! Imagine my surprise when I heard from Sir Cameron Mackintosh that mine was his third request in that week!

I am therefore deeply grateful to everyone who has contributed to this book. To be pestered for a recipe when in the middle of a run of a play, learning lines, filming, probably staying away from home, must have been a nuisance. The response to my letters has been marvellous.

There are so many people - friends, family, strangers - who have helped financially and made practical comments and given inspiration without whom this book would not have been produced.

I would particularly like to thank Katherine Spring for doing all the illustrations, Ted and Lyn Rockley for designing the cover, Jilly Dolphin for all the typesetting and Jill Roche, Joan Rose and Debbie Spring for help and encouragement in times of need. They have all been wonderful!

I hope you will enjoy reading and using the recipes and persuade all your friends to buy a copy.

Margaret Maughan

ALL ROYALTIES FROM THIS PUBLICATION WILL GO TO THE SOPHIE WINTER MEMORIAL FUND

3

THE SOPHIE WINTER
MEMORIAL TRUST

The Trust has been set up to commemorate and celebrate the life and work of a young actress who died in June 1995 from a misdiagnosed ectopic pregnancy just before her final performance in Alan Ayckbourn's newly written play 'A Word From Our Sponsor' at the Stephen Joseph Theatre, Scarborough.

Alan Ayckbourn in his newspaper tribute to Sophie wrote: "Hers was a talent I needed and loved. I had hoped that in return I could have had a part in encouraging and nurturing that talent through a few more plays together. I think we would both have enjoyed that."

It is appropriate then that the purpose of the Trust is to try to do just that; to commission new plays and have them produced. Already our first commissioned new play, 'Fool to Yourself' by Robert Shearman, has been premiered very successfully at the Stephen Joseph Theatre. More new plays, hopefully, will follow.

The Trust is also strongly associated with the work of the Ectopic Pregnancy Support Network which can be contacted through the Miscarriage Association on 01924 200799.
For further information about the Trust please write to:-
The Administrator, 31 Oxhey Road, Watford WD1 4QG

John Winter
Administrator

CONTENTS

BREAKFAST
AND
BRUNCH

RAY COONEY'S LEMON SQUASH

**Recipe sent by
Ray Cooney**

Ingredients
4 lemons
50 g (2 oz) citric acid
900 g (2 lbs) sugar

Method
Put the citric acid, sugar and zest of the 4 lemons into a large heatproof
jug. Add 12 cups of boiling water and leave to cool. When cool add the
juice of the 4 lemons. Use as a squash and dilute to taste. It lasts for
ages.

Note
Ray Cooney always has his own 'secret' jug hidden away for his own
use. Sometimes he lets his wife partake - but only when he's feeling
especially generous!

Drawback
Everybody adores it and it is difficult to resist offering it to anyone who
calls. It is particularly popular with plumbers, electricians and
maintenance men of all kinds!

DELICIOUS BREAKFAST DRINK

Recipe sent by
Stephanie Beecham

Stephanie says:

"I am a disinterested cook BUT breakfast must be swallowed so for a good supply of energy I throw:

1 banana
a handful of soft fruit - usually strawberries
orange juice

into a blender and make a delicious drink with a texture perfect for swallowing vitamin pills".

ORIENTAL FRUIT COMPÔTE WITH HONEY AND GINGER YOGHURT

Recipe sent by
Maureen Lipman

Ingredients

100 g (4 oz) dried apricots   100 g (4 oz) dried Californian prunes
100 g (4 oz) dried figs   50 g (2 oz) plump sultanas
½ teaspoon ground cinnamon
100 g (4 oz) stoned semi-dried Californian dates
100 g (4 oz) kumquats, sliced   100 g (4 oz) bottled Morello cherries
1 teaspoon rosewater   juice of 1 orange
1 teaspoon orange zest   50 g (2 oz) roasted, peeled almonds

For the yoghurt

275 ml (½ pint) Greek yoghurt
1 tablespoon clear orange blossom honey
2 tablespoons stem ginger, finely chopped

Method

Put the apricots, prunes, figs and sultanas in a serving bowl, add the cinnamon, cover with water and place in the fridge for one day. Add the dates, kumquats, cherries and rosewater. Pour over the orange juice and stir in the zest. Flavour the yoghurt with the honey, stir in the ginger and pour into a serving bowl. Just before serving sprinkle the roasted almonds over the compôte.

SCRAMBLED EGGS

Recipe sent by
Sir Richard Eyre

Ingredients

Serves 2

4 eggs
100 g (4 oz) butter
pepper to season

Method

Melt slightly salted butter over a low heat. Whisk the eggs in a bowl with a fork. They need to be lightly whisked so the yolks and whites are mixed but not frothed as for an omelette. When the butter is melted, add the eggs, keep stirring and cook very, very slowly. The Roux brothers recommend cooking over a steamer and stirring for 20 minutes. Sir Richard is not such an extremist!

Note

"Perfect scrambled eggs should be moist, fluffy and entirely unadulterated. It's one of the great dishes of the world", says Sir Richard.

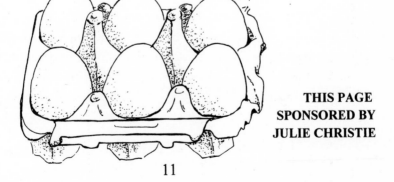

**THIS PAGE
SPONSORED BY
JULIE CHRISTIE**

BRAIN FOOD

Recipe sent by
Philip Bird

Ingredients   Serves 4
200-250 g (8-12 oz) smoked mackerel
1 large onion
200 g (8 oz) brown rice or more if Philip is invited
a few mushrooms and/or sweetcorn

Method
Peel the skin off the fish and put into a frying pan over a very slow heat.
The oil comes out after about 10 minutes and you don't need any
cooking oil. Add the finely chopped onion and while it's cooking wash
the rice thousands of times and put it on to cook. Add the chopped
mushrooms and sweetcorn to the fish, stir and cover. By the time the
rice is ready the fish will be as well. Drain and rinse the rice and add it
to the fish mixture. Stir it in. Serve with a knob of butter if you're
feeling prosperous and perhaps a raw carrot.

Note
Philip says : "Ever since I read that eating oily fish like herring, mackerel
and kippers is good for the brain, I have been trying to find a way to get
my young family to eat it! I hit on this incredibly simple meal which
they at least find tolerable". As this is a variation of a kedgeree it can be
served for breakfast or brunch as well as other meals.

BEST SANDWICH EVER

Recipe sent by
Victoria Wood

Ingredients
Two big slices of wholemeal bread, preferably with bits in
Bits of butter to spread on them
Lots of avocado, tomato, cucumber, cress
(Alfafa sprouts too if you live in one of the three places that sell
them!)

Method
Put it all together. (**PUT THE BREAD ON THE OUTSIDE.**)
Put real mayonnaise, salt and pepper in the middle.
EAT IT!

COCKLES

Recipe sent by
Julie Walters

Ingredients
¼ pint fresh cockles
2 slices of wholemeal bread
butter
freshly ground pepper

Method
Butter the bread, place the cockles on one piece, cover with the other piece, open mouth, shove in, clamp teeth down on bread and masticate - OK?

CHEESE CRISPIES

Recipe sent by
Jane Asher

Ingredients

Makes 30 biscuits

85 g (3 oz) plain flour
¼ teaspoon celery salt
60 g (2 oz) unsalted butter
60 g (2 oz) mature Cheddar cheese, grated
1 egg, size 3, beaten
30 g (1 oz) Parmesan cheese, finely grated

A 5 cm (2 inch) plain cutter

Method

Set the oven at 230°C (450°F) gas mark 8. Sift the flour and salt into a bowl, rub in the batter and add the Cheddar cheese. Work the mixture together to form a dough and chill for 2 hours. Cut off small pieces of the dough and roll out thinly on a lightly floured surface. Cut out the biscuits using the cutter and place on greased baking trays. Brush with beaten egg and sprinkle with Parmesan cheese. Bake for 5 minutes until golden. Leave to cool on the trays for a minute before transferring to a wire rack to finish cooling.

Note

These feather-light, melt-in-the-mouth biscuits will keep for up to two days stored in an airtight container and kept in the fridge.

BLUEBERRY MUFFINS

Recipe sent by
Sir Paul McCartney

Ingredients   Makes 18
¼ cup (40 g / 1½ oz) sugar
3 cups (350 g / 12 oz) self raising flour
½ teaspoon salt
1½ cups (340 ml/12 fl oz) milk
1 egg
4 tablespoons (50 g/2 oz) butter or margarine
1½ cups (225 g/8 oz) blueberries or berries of your choice

Method
Preheat the oven to 200°C (400°F) gas mark 6 and lightly grease two
trays of muffin tins. Grease a large mixing bowl, then mix the sugar,
flour and salt in it. Beat the milk and egg in a small bowl and pour it
into the centre of the dry mix. Stir briefly. Melt the butter, add it to the
batter mixture and stir well. Drain the berries if frozen and sprinkle a
little flour to coat each one. Fresh berries can be used. Add them to the
batter and stir well. Spoon the batter into the muffin tins and bake for
20-25 minutes until lightly golden on top.

Note
These gorgeous muffins are a treat at any time, but particularly for a
relaxed weekend breakfast. Serve with butter and honey. The recipe is
from *Linda McCartney's Home Cooking* published by Arcade
Publishing, New York.

D J'S PLUM SAUCE

Recipe sent by
David Jason OBE

Ingredients

2 kilos (4½ lbs) red plums, halved and stoned

6 onions, chopped

100g (4 oz) salt

50 g (2 oz) mustard powder

10 g (½ oz) chillies

25 g (1 oz) allspice

a pinch of nutmeg

2.2 litres (4 pints) vinegar

450 g (1 lb) sugar

225 g (8 oz) sultanas

25 g (1 oz) whole ginger, chopped

10 g (½ oz) turmeric

Method

Put the plums, onions, sultanas, chillies and crushed ginger with half the vinegar in a large pan. Bring to the boil then simmer for 30 minutes. Strain and return the solids to the pan with the mustard, sugar, salt, nutmeg, allspice and turmeric. Add the remaining vinegar and simmer for 30-40 minutes. Bottle and keep for at least a month before eating.

Note

David Jason says: "In an endeavour to make use of own-grown plums, this is a lovely sauce to have with hot or cold food or as a special ingredient to other dishes".

SOUPS
AND
STARTERS

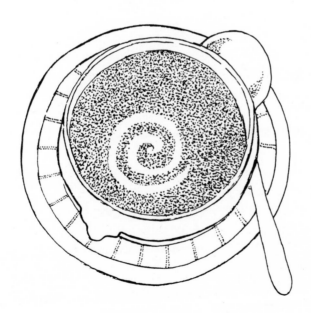

BORTSCH SOUP

Recipe sent by
Twiggy Lawson

Ingredients   Serves 4
455 g (1 lb) beetroot
2 medium potatoes (about 115 g/4 oz when mashed)
1 medium onion   2 tablespoons lemon juice
salt and freshly ground black pepper
570 ml (1 pint/20 fl oz) vegetable stock or water
140 ml (5 fl oz/¼ pint) sour cream
For the garnish
4 tablespoons freshly chopped chives   sour cream (optional)

Method
Cook the beetroot until tender then peel and slice. Boil the potatoes and mash them. Put the cooked beetroot, mashed potato, chopped onion and lemon juice into a blender or processor and purée. Add salt and pepper, stock and sour cream and purée for a further minute. Place the soup in the fridge and chill for 1 hour, then pour into individual serving dishes and sprinkle a little chopped chives or parsley on top to garnish, followed by a dollop of sour cream if desired.

Note
This soup is one of Twiggy's favourites and can be eaten cold or hot in which case reheat rather than chill. The recipe is from *'Linda McCartney's Home Cooking'* and is her variation of the traditional rich Russian peasant soup.

CELERY AND LOVAGE SOUP

Recipe sent by
Michelle Newell

Ingredients   Serves 6-8
2 heads celery
1 medium sized potato, peeled and cut into dice
1 large onion, chopped
25 g (1 oz) butter
1¼ litres (2 pints) chicken stock (home-made if possible)
or vegetable stock
a handful of lovage leaves, chopped
salt and pepper
Garnish
Cream or crème fraîche (optional)
a handful of chopped chives

Method
Cut off the base and ½ inch from the tops of the celery. Discard the
yellow inside leaves as they are bitter. Wash the stalks, destring and cut
into 1 inch pieces and chop the bright green leaves. Melt the butter in
a heavy bottomed pan over a low heat. Add the celery, onion and
potato and sweat, covered, for 10 minutes until the onion is transparent.
Do not allow this to brown. Next add the stock and bring slowly to the
boil, skimming off any scum with a perforated spoon. Add the finely
chopped lovage and simmer until the vegetables are tender. Take off the
heat and leave to cool.

Put in a blender (not a processor or mixture will not be fine enough) and return to pan to reheat. Check seasoning (less salt needed if bouillon is used). Serve in heated bowls with a dollop of cream or crème fraîche if desired. Sprinkle with chopped chives.

Note

Lovage is an old fashioned herb that has recently made a come-back; it can now be found on supermarket shelves in the summer months, but it is easy to grow in a large pot. It is a highly aromatic member of the celery family and adds a warm spiciness to this soup, while enhancing the flavour of celery. Wonderful sprinkled on salads too!

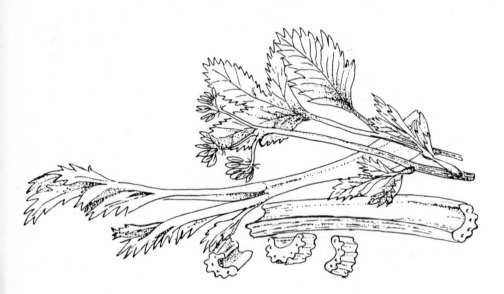

RICHARD WILSON'S CULLEN SKINK

Recipe sent by
Richard Wilson

Ingredients   Serves 4
1 kilo (2 lbs) smoked haddock
1 large onion, sliced
875 ml (1½ lb) mashed potatoes
50 g (2 oz) butter
a little cream
850 ml (1½ pints) milk

Method
Peel and boil the potatoes, drain and mash them. Put the fish in a pan
with water just sufficient to cover it. Simmer for about 5 minutes.
Remove the fish, and take out the bones and remove the skin. Return
it to the pan with the sliced onion and continue cooking a further 15
minutes. Add the milk and bring to the boil. Then add the mashed
potato - more can be added for a thicker soup. Stir to a creamy
consistency. Cut the butter into small pieces and add to the soup.
Season to taste and add a little cream before serving.

Note
Cullen Skink is a very rich, tasty Scottish soup. This recipe makes 4
good portions.

CARROT AND CORIANDER SOUP

Recipe sent by
The New Covent Garden Soup Company

Ingredients   Serves 6
25 g (1oz) butter
1 medium onion, finely chopped
1 garlic clove, crushed
550 g (1¼ lb) carrots of which 450 g (1 lb) roughly chopped
100 g (4 oz) coarsely grated
1 litre (1¾ pints) vegetable stock
pinch freshly grated nutmeg
1 tablespoon chopped fresh coriander
150 ml (¼ pint) single cream
salt and freshly ground black pepper

To garnish
150 ml (¼ pint) yoghurt   2 tablespoons chopped fresh coriander

Method
Melt the butter and cook the onion and garlic gently until soft, in a
covered saucepan, without colouring. Add the roughly chopped
carrots, stock and nutmeg. Cover, bring to the boil and simmer gently
until the vegetables are tender. Cool a little, then purée in a liquidiser.
Return to a clean saucepan and stir in the grated carrots, coriander and
cream. Taste for seasoning. Serve garnished with a swirl of yoghurt and
a sprinkling of chopped fresh coriander.

CHILLED TOMATO SOUP

Recipe sent by
Nigel Hawthorne

Ingredients
2 x 400g (14 oz) cans of tomatoes
1 garlic clove
a few fresh basil leaves (or a little dried)
2 teaspoons lemon juice
1 teaspoon sugar
salt and pepper
2 cartons soured cream

Method
Put into the blender ½ can tomatoes together with lemon juice, sugar, basil, salt and pepper and the garlic crushed with a little salt. Blend until quite smooth. Add the rest of the tomatoes with their juice and blend again. Next blend in the soured cream. When it's smooth and creamy check for seasoning. Adjust if necessary. Pour into a bowl or separate bowls and cover. Refrigerate until very cold.

Note
Nigel Hawthorne says this is a mystery recipe as he is dubious about the source but it goes without saying that it will be absolutely delicious as you can't fail with tomatoes and basil. He is a tiny bit apprehensive of adding this in the company of Delia Smith but is sure even she would understand that there's always room for experiment!

TARTE AUX ASPERGES

Recipe sent by
Marcia Warren
Serves 4-6

Ingredients

For the pastry
225g (8 oz) plain flour
a pinch of salt
175g (6oz) butter

For the filling
a 900g (2 lb) bunch of asparagus
425 ml (¾ pint) béchamel sauce
50g (2 oz) grated cheese

For the sauce
25 g (1 oz) plain flour
25 g (1 oz) butter
425 ml (¾ pint) milk
seasoning

Method

Make the pastry by kneading the flour and butter together and adding a little water to make a paste. Leave to rest for 1 hour if possible. Prepare the asparagus very carefully by peeling off the dry outer skin from the stalks. Put them tied in a bunch and heads uppermost, into boiling salted water to which you also add a lump of sugar. Cook for 20 minutes or longer if very large. Drain and cut each one into 3-4 pieces, discarding the hard part at the ends. Roll out the pastry and line a flat buttered pie tin with it. Cover with greaseproof paper and fill with baking beans to keep the pastry flat. Bake in a hot oven for 20 minutes. Remove the paper and beans. Make the sauce - put the milk, flour and butter in a saucepan and bring to the boil, whisking all the time. When it has thickened leave to cook slowly for 3-4 minutes on a very low heat. Season well with salt, pepper and nutmeg. Add the grated cheese and asparagus off the heat, then pour into the pastry case. Return to the oven until brown. Serve very hot. **DIVINE!**

MUSHROOM TART

Recipe sent by
Peter Forbes

Ingredients

250 g (9 oz) mushrooms, wiped (go for dark brown, medium
cupped or field mushrooms)
50 g (2 oz) butter, softened, not melted
2 cloves garlic
2 tablespoons chopped parsley
175 g (6 oz) puff pastry, defrosted

Method

Preheat the oven to 220°C (425°F) gas mark 7. Cut the mushrooms into bite sized pieces. Mix the butter with the crushed garlic. Fry the mushrooms in a shallow pan with half the butter, adding a little more butter or olive oil if it gets soaked up. Stir in the parsley. On a lightly floured surface roll the pastry into a rectangle approximately 20 x 13 cm (8 x 5 inches). Lift carefully onto a baking sheet. Using a sharp knife score a small rectangle 4 cm (1½ inches) from the edge, cutting only halfway through the pastry. Scoop the mushrooms from the pan and place them on the innermost rectangle, trying not to let them hang over the outer rim. Place in a hot oven and bake for 15 minutes until the pastry is risen. Dot with the remaining butter then close the door for another 5-7 minutes until the pastry is golden and the mushrooms sizzling. Serve straight from the oven, before the pastry has time to go soggy.

Note

Peter says: "I am a fairly simple cook and tend to follow recipes slavishly, but was delighted to discover this one as it is both simple and extremely delicious and makes an ideal vegetarian alternative to a Sunday roast or steak pie." The recipe is from Nigel Slater's *'The 30-Minute Cook'* published by Michael Joseph and Penguin Books 1994.

DRIZZLED STILTON MUSHROOMS

Recipe sent by
Michael Simkins

Ingredients
2 large flat mushrooms per person
a large block of Stilton cheese

Method
Carefully wash the mushrooms. Upturn them and lay them on a grill pan. Grate the Stilton onto the mushrooms. Place under a medium grill and wait a few minutes until the cheese has melted. Remove and serve immediately.

Note
"The combination of the raw mushrooms and the drizzled cheese is yummy on the palate and provides an excellent and extremely easy starter to a main meal", says Michael.

OVEN BAKED WILD MUSHROOM RISOTTO

Recipe sent by Delia Smith
As a starter serves 6

Ingredients

1 x 10 g (½ oz) packet dried porcini
225 g (8 oz) fresh dark grilled mushrooms
60 g (2½ oz) butter
175 g (6 oz) Italian canaroli rice (risotto rice)
150 ml (5 fl oz) dry Madeira
2 tablespoons parmesan (Parmigiano Reggiano) freshly grated
   plus 50 g (2 oz) extra shaved into flakes
salt and black pepper

Method

You will need a 23 cm (9 inches) shallow ovenproof dish, approximately 5 cm (2 inches) deep. Preheat the oven to 150°C (300°F) gas mark 2. First of all you need to soak the dried mushrooms by placing them in a bowl and pour 570 ml (1 pint) boiling water over them. Leave them for ½ hour. Meanwhile chop the fresh mushrooms into 1 cm (½ inch) chunks. Now melt the butter in a medium saucepan, add the onion and let it cook over a gentle heat for about 5 minutes. Then add the fresh mushrooms, stir well and leave on one side. Place a sieve lined with a double piece of absorbent kitchen paper over a bowl and strain the porcini, reserving the liquid. Squeeze any excess liquid out, then chop them finely and add to the other mushrooms and onion. Keep the heat low and let them sweat gently for about 20 minutes. Put the dish in the oven to warm. Now add the rice and stir it around, then add the Madeira followed by the strained soaking liquid. Add a level teaspoon of salt and some freshly milled black pepper, bring to simmering point, then transfer the whole lot to the warmed dish. Place in the centre of the oven without covering. Set the timer and give it 20 minutes exactly.

After that gently stir in the grated Parmesan, turning the rice grains over. Now give it a further 15 minutes, then remove from the oven and cover with a clean tea towel. Serve 'presto pronto' on warmed plates and sprinkle with shavings of Parmesan.

Note

Delia Smith says : "I've always loved real Italian risotto, a creamy mass with the rice grains 'al dente' - but oh, the bother of all that stirring to make it. Then one day I was making a good old fashioned rice pudding and I thought, why not try a risotto in the oven? Why not indeed - it works like a dream and leaves you in peace to enjoy the company of your friends while it is cooking. I have since discovered, in fact, that in Liguria they do make a special kind of baked risotto called 'arrosto' so my version turns out to be quite authentic after all."

The recipe is copyright Delia Smith 1995 and is from *'Delia Smith's Winter Collection'* (published by BBC Books).

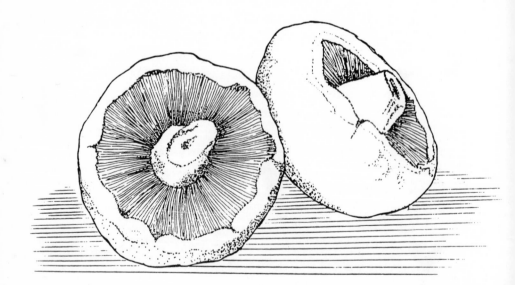

COURGETTE SOUFFLÉ

Recipe sent by
Maria Friedman

Serves 4

Ingredients

Soufflé

340 g (¾ lb) courgettes
25 g (1 oz) butter
22 g (¾ oz) butter
120 ml (4 fl oz) milk
1 rounded + 1 level dessertspoon plain flour
salt, pepper, nutmeg to taste
2 eggs

Tomato cream sauce

250 g (7 oz) tinned tomatoes
120 ml (3 fl oz) sour cream
sugar, salt, pepper, basil
Parmesan cheese

Method

Finely grate the courgettes, sprinkle with salt and leave in a colander for 30 minutes then rinse, drain and dry them. Melt 25 g (1 oz) butter and sauté the courgettes for 5-8 minutes. Melt the 22 g (¾ oz) butter in a saucepan, stir in the flour off the heat, add the milk, bring to the boil and simmer for 3 minutes, stirring continuously to make a thick white sauce. Cool slightly and add the egg yolks, stirring well. Season and stir in the courgettes. Whisk the whites until stiff and fold into the sauce gently. Pour the mixture into a greased savarin or similar mould and stand in a roasting tin with water to come about halfway up the sides of the mould. Cook for 20 - 25 minutes at 180°C (350°F) gas mark 4. Meanwhile make the sauce - mix the tomatoes, sour cream and seasoning and simmer until reduced and thickened. Turn out the soufflé and pour the sauce over. Sprinkle with Parmesan and put back into the oven for 15 minutes until crisp on top. BON APPETIT!

FISH

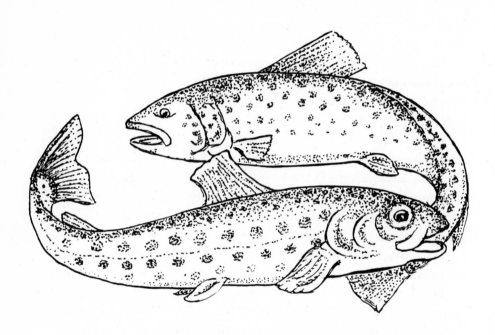

WHITBY FISH PIE

Recipe sent by
Rebecca Johnson

Ingredients

Serves 4

2 smoked mackerel fillets - chopped
1 kilo (2 lbs) potatoes - cooked and mashed
200g (8 oz) mushrooms - sliced
2 leeks - sliced
2 carrots - grated
25 g (1 oz) butter
175 - 200 g (6 - 8 oz) grated Cheddar cheese
1 teaspoon dried tarragon

Method

Boil, drain and mash the potatoes. Melt the butter in a pan and fry the mushrooms, leeks and tarragon. Plunge the grated carrots into boiling water and simmer for 1-2 minutes then drain well. Mix together the fish, potato, mushroom mixture, carrots and half the cheese. Place in a buttered dish. Sprinkle the remaining cheese on top and brown in the oven or under a hot grill.

Note

The top can be decorated with large prawns and fresh dill if you wish.

FISH BAKED IN THE OVEN

Recipe sent by
Sîan Phillips

Ingredients Serves 4

½ kilo (about 1 lb) haddock or cod fillets
salt, pepper, celery powder, curry powder for seasoning
4 carrots
1 clove garlic
2 green peppers
2 apples
1 dessertspoon lemon juice
50 g (2 oz) margarine

Method

Preheat the oven to 190°C (375° F) gas mark 5. Clean the fish and sprinkle with the seasoning and lemon juice. Clean and grate the carrots. Peel and slice the apples and de-seed and slice the peppers. Crush and chop the garlic. Put the apples in a greased fireproof dish. Add the garlic, peppers and carrots and lay the fish on top. Dab the margarine all over. Cover and bake for about half an hour.

Note

This is a quick and easy dish which can be served with rice or potatoes.

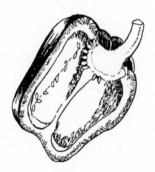
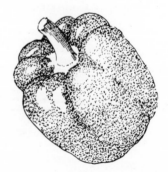

SALMON IN PASTRY WITH GINGER AND CURRANTS

Recipe sent by
Steven Pacey

Ingredients   Serves 4

675 g - 1 kilo (1½ - 2 lbs) fresh salmon   salt and pepper
2-3 pieces preserved ginger   1 tablespoon currants
50 g (2 oz) slightly salted butter   225 g (8 oz) shortcrust pastry
egg for egg wash

Method

Fillet the salmon and skin it. Remove any internal bones with a pair of
pliers. Divide the fish into two horizontal slices. Season with salt and
pepper. Rinse the ginger of its syrup. Chop it finely and mix with the
currants and softened butter. Spread over each slice of fish. Sandwich
the fish together. Roll out the pastry and wrap it around the fish to
make a neat parcel. Egg wash the pastry and bake for 30 - 45 minutes,
depending on size and shape of finished product. Cook for 20 minutes
at 220C (425F) gas mark 7, then reduce to 150C (300F) gas mark 2, for
the remainder of the time. Serve with herb and cream sauce.

Note

This is one of Steven's favourite recipes which his wife cooks for him.
It is a creation of Joyce Molyneux who runs the 'Carved Angel' in
Dartmouth. The recipe is from *Take Twelve Cooks* by Kay Avila, a
Channel 4 book published by Thames-Macdonald 1986.

HERB AND CREAM SAUCE

**Recipe sent by
Steven Pacey**

Ingredients

Serves 4

2 shallots
25 g (1 oz) butter
4 teaspoons chopped parsley
2 teaspoons chopped chervil
2 teaspoons tarragon
1 teaspoon flour
300 ml (½ pint) single cream
1 teaspoon coarse mustard
1 egg yolk
squeezed lemon juice
salt and pepper

Method

Chop the shallots and sweat in a little butter; add the herbs and cook a
little longer. Add the flour, mixing well, and then the single cream.
Bring gently to the boil, stirring well with a wooden spoon. Cook for
3 minutes. Season and add the mustard, egg yolk and lemon juice then
recheck the seasoning. Serve with the salmon in pastry.

Note

This sauce was created by Joyce Molyneux to serve with the previous
recipe, Salmon in Pastry, and is also from *'Take Twelve Cooks'*.

SALMON FISHCAKES

Recipe sent by
Michael Bryant

Ingredients
1 large can red salmon, drained and skin removed
4 medium potatoes (ideally Desirée), peeled
2 shallots, finely chopped
1 heaped tablespoon tomato purée
1 good handful chopped parsley
salt and freshly ground pepper
seasoned flour

Method
First boil the potatoes, drain and mash well. Add the salmon, shallots, tomato purée, salt and pepper and parsley. Mix well with a fork or hands. Form into 6-8 cakes and coat with seasoned flour. Fry in good oil for 5-8 minutes each side until brown. Best served with baked beans!

Note
This is Michael's mother's recipe which she often made with pink salmon when they were hard up. Michael says he has eaten fish cakes in the best of restaurants but has always been disappointed. Tinned salmon gives that special flavour that is superior to fresh salmon when used in fish cakes.

TUNA FISH SALAD

Recipe sent by
Gabrielle Drake

Ingredients   Serves 4
2 x 198 g (7 oz) tins tuna fish
6 eggs, hard boiled
3 sharp apples
a few toasted almond flakes
3 tomatoes
2 generous tablespoons home-made mayonnaise
1 heaped teaspoon tomato purée
1 small teaspoon curry powder

Method
Mix together the mayonnaise, curry powder, tomato purée, diced apple
and sliced hard boiled eggs. Drain the tuna fish and break into chunks.
Combine with the other ingredients. Transfer to a serving dish and
garnish with wedges of tomato and toasted almonds.

GENERAL GRUDGER

Recipe sent by
Richard Griffiths

Ingredients
Serves 4

25 g (1 oz) sultanas

3 tablespoons milk

1 kilo (2 lbs) potatoes

50 g (2 oz) butter

salt/pepper

3 tablespoons mango chutney

100 g (4 oz) grated Cheddar cheese

500 g (1 lb) large prawns

4 tablespoons breadcrumbs

a little extra butter

2 tablespoons curry powder

2 tablespoons finely chopped parsley

Method
Soak the sultanas in milk while you boil the potatoes, then peel and mash them with half of the butter. Grease a pie or gratin dish with the rest of the butter. Spread a third of the potato over the bottom, then put in the chutney, half the cheese, half the remaining potato, then the prawns, then the rest of the cheese and top with the remaining potato. Fry the breadcrumbs in a little extra butter then mix in the curry powder, sultanas and parsley. Make a well in the centre of the dish and pour in the spicy crumbs. Bake in the preheated oven - 190°C (375°F) gas mark 5, until heated through for about ½ hour.

Note
This favourite luncheon/supper dish of Richard Griffiths is an Anglo Indian curiosity found in a copy of a cookery book published in 1910 in Allahabad. It makes a cheerful family lunch. Richard adds 3 hard boiled eggs and uses extra large prawns.

STIR FRY EXPRESS PIZZA

Recipe sent by
Claire Daniels

Ingredients

Serves 2

2 tablespoons olive oil
2 heaped tablespoons crème fraîche
2 medium carrots
2 medium leeks
a garlic clove, finely chopped
2 x medium (20 cm) or 1 x large (30cm) pizza bases
100 g (4 oz) cooked, peeled prawns (thawed)
50 g (2 oz) grated Parmesan or Cheddar cheese
salt and pepper

Method

Preheat the oven to 220°C (425°F) gas mark 7. Cut the carrots into ribbons using a vegetable peeler. Cut the leeks thinly, diagonally. Heat the oil in a frying pan and fry the garlic, carrots and leeks until softened. Season with salt and pepper. Place the pizza bases onto a baking sheet, cover with crème fraîche, then with the cooked vegetables. Top with the prawns, sprinkle with cheese and season well. Bake for 12 - 15 minutes until the base is crisp and golden and the cheese has melted. NO PROBLEM.

Note

'Get a video, open the vino, light the fire and enjoy', says Claire.

THIS PAGE
SPONSORED BY
McCAIN FOODS LTD

SALMON FISHCAKES WITH SORREL SAUCE

Recipe sent by
Melvin Schnable

Ingredients

Serves 6

450 g (1 lb) dry mashed potatoes
1 tablespoon Dijon mustard
2 teaspoons lemon juice
salt and pepper to taste

450 g (1 lb) salmon fillet, skinned
2 tablespoons Worcestershire sauce
50 g (2 oz) plain flour

For the sauce

75 g (3 oz) shallots, finely chopped
few parsley stalks, chopped
225 g (8 fl oz) double cream
150 ml (¼ pint) white wine
75 g (3 oz) flour
dill sprigs for garnish

1 bay leaf
½ tablespoon black peppercorns
570 ml (1 pint) water
75 g (3 oz) butter
4 tablespoons sorrel,
    picked and shredded

Method

Apart from the butter, cream and sorrel, simmer all the ingredients for the sauce for about 30 minutes or until reduced by half. When ready pass through a fine sieve. Place salmon on a deep tray and pour over the stock. Cover and place in a moderate oven, 180°C (350°F) gas mark 4, and cook until firm to touch - about 20 minutes. Remove salmon from the stock and keep warm. Reserve stock. In a pan melt the butter and slowly add the flour, stir over a low heat for about 5 minutes. Add the fish stock slowly whisking continuously and cook for about 10 - 15 minutes. Pass through a fine sieve, return to pan, add double cream, sorrel, salt and pepper to taste. Cook until a coating consistency is achieved. Keep hot for serving.

For the fishcakes, mix the mashed potato, salmon, mustard, lemon juice and Worcestershire sauce in mixing bowl, making sure the salmon is broken into small flakes. Mould the mixture into 6 cakes, roll them in the remaining flour to coat and prevent sticking. Shallow pan fry until brown, then transfer to an oven to bake for a further 10 - 15 minutes, 230°C (450°F) gas mark 8 until hot in the middle. To serve, flood plates with the sorrel sauce, place the fishcakes on top and garnish with dill sprigs.

Note

This is one of Melvin Schnable's favourite recipes from the Mezzanine at the Royal National Theatre.

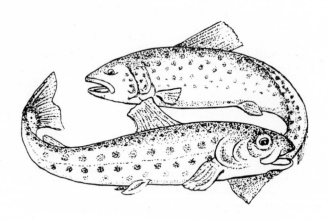

GRILLED SCALLOPS, AVOCADO-CORN RELISH AND CORIANDER OIL

Recipe sent by
Anthony Worrall Thompson

Tortilla topped with corn relish

2 Haas avocadoes, peeled, seeded and mashed
1 corn on the cob, blanched, chargrilled and nibs removed
1 chilli, finely diced
¼ teaspoon coriander powder
¼ teaspoon cumin powder
1 small red onion, finely diced
2 plum tomatoes, seeded and diced
½ bunch coriander leaves finely chopped
juice of 1 lemon
2 tablespoons olive oil
salt and ground black pepper
Combine all the ingredients. Do not place in a food processor. IT SHOULD BE CHUNKY. Season to taste.

Tortilla

1 packet supermarket flour tortillas
150 ml (¼ pint) corn oil
salt and ground black pepper
Rip each tortilla into 5 jagged pieces. Do not cut into neat triangles. Fry in hot corn oil until golden and crispy, drain on kitchen paper. Season and set aside in an airtight plastic container until ready for use.

Scallops

1 large diver-caught scallop per person, cut in two horizontally, cooked in butter for 30 seconds each side just prior to serving.

Coriander Oil

2 bunches coriander, leaves only
570 ml (1 pint) extra virgin olive oil

Blanch the coriander leaves in boiling water for 30 seconds and refresh in iced cold water. Squeeze dry. Blend the leaves and olive oil in a food processor and put in a bottle. Shake well before use.

Presentation

2 pieces of tortilla at 10pm and 2pm topped with salsa and half a scallop. Dribble some thick coriander oil around the plate.

VEGETARIAN

LENTIL FLAN WITH COURGETTES

Recipe sent by
Christine Wall

Ingredients

Serves 4-6

Case

100 g (4 oz) lentils
1 tablespoon olive oil
1 onion, chopped
1 tablespoon tomato purée
50 g (2 oz) porridge oats
1 tablespoon lemon juice
2 tablespoons chopped herbs

Filling

200 g (8 oz) courgettes
2 eggs, beaten
1 tablespoon cornflour
2 fl oz (55 mls) milk
50 g (2 oz) grated cheese

Method

Cook the lentils in just enough water to make them thick and mushy. Cook the onions in a little oil then combine them with the rest of the case ingredients. Press into a flan tin or dish across the bottom and up the sides. Wash and slice the courgettes. Beat the eggs, milk and cornflour together and add the grated cheese. Season. Put the courgettes into the case, then pour the liquid over them. Cook until set in the preheated oven - 200°C (400°F) gas mark 6 for 20-30 minutes.

Note

Christine suggests experimenting with different fillings. The flan could be served with a home-made tomato sauce.

HOME-MADE TOMATO SAUCE

Recipe sent by
Sir Paul McCartney

Ingredients
1 tablespoon olive oil
1 clove garlic, crushed
1 onion, chopped
1 400g (1 lb) can chopped tomatoes
1 small can tomato paste
½ cup tomato juice
1 teaspoon oregano
salt and freshly ground black pepper

Method
Heat the olive oil in a saucepan, add the garlic and onion and sauté lightly. Add the remaining ingredients and stir well. Bring to the boil, reduce the heat and simmer, covered, for 30 minutes. Stir occasionally.

Note
This recipe is from Paul McCartney's wife's book *'Linda McCartney's Home Cooking'*.

COLCANNON

**Recipe sent by
Sinead Cusack**

Ingredients
6 - 8 potatoes
50 - 100 g (2 - 4 oz) butter
1 head cabbage
1½ cups milk (approx)
salt and pepper

Method
Peel the potatoes and boil in salted water. Quarter core and finely shred the cabbage. Boil rapidly in a little salted water, stirring occasionally until cooked and the water evaporated. Mash the cooked potatoes with the milk and stir in the cabbage immediately and beat very well. Taste for seasoning. Serve in a warm dish, hollowing the centre a little and put the butter in the hollow to melt into the vegetables.

Note
This is a meal the Cusack family always had given to them by their mother on the night of Halloween - whether it's an Irish tradition or one familiar to all 'trick or treaters', Sinead Cusack doesn't know.

MACARONI CHEESE

**Recipe sent by
Sheila Hancock**

Ingredients

Serves 4

570 ml (1 pint) milk infused with:-
½ onion, peeled
6 whole peppercorns
2 bay leaves
1 teaspoon thyme
½ teaspoon grated nutmeg

salt and freshly ground black pepper
50 g (2 oz) butter
25 g (1 oz) flour
175 g (6 oz) wholewheat macaroni
175 g (6 oz) grated Cheddar cheese
1 tablespoon freshly chopped parsley

Method

First infuse the milk by adding the onion, spices and herbs and bringing it just to the boil. Remove from the heat, cover and allow to stand for 10-15 minutes, then strain it. Meanwhile, melt the butter over a gentle heat. Add the flour and cook this roux for 2-3 minutes, stirring occasionally. Cook the macaroni in plenty of boiling salted water for 8-10 minutes. When it is cooked, drain and put it into a warm serving dish. Quickly stir 110 g (4 oz) of the cheese and the parsley into the sauce, then pour this over the macaroni. Cover with the remaining cheese and grill for 5-7 minutes until the cheese is bubbling and golden. Serve straight away.

Note

The first mention of Macaroni Cheese being eaten in England was in 1720 and it is hardly surprising that it is still popular today as it is both wholesome and tasty. It can be adapted very easily to suit wholewheat pasta and wholewheat flour can be used for the sauce. As this combination produces a darker coloured dish add extra colour by using plenty of chopped parsley. This can be served with salad or steamed green vegetables for lunch or a light supper. The recipe is from *'Sarah Brown's Vegetarian Kitchen'* published by the BBC in 1984.

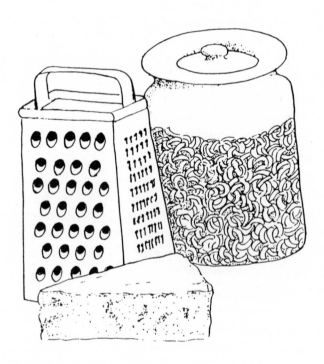

TOYAH'S AUBERGINE AND BEAN LAYER BAKE

Recipe sent by
Toyah Wilcox

Ingredients
Serves 4 - 6

1 kg (2 lbs) aubergines, sliced
400 g (14 oz) can white kidney beans, drained
2 tablespoons oil   1 onion, chopped finely
250 g (8 oz) Mozzarella cheese, sliced
2 cloves garlic, chopped   800 g (1¾ lb) can peeled tomatoes
5 g (2 oz) Parmesan cheese, grated
2 bay leaves   2 teaspoons dried oregano
50 g (2 oz) fresh bread crumbs   salt and pepper

Method
Sprinkle the aubergines with salt and set aside. Heat the oil in a pan, add the onion and garlic and sauté until golden. Add the tomatoes with their juice, bay leaves and oregano and simmer for about 25 minutes, until thickened. Season well. Rinse the aubergines then cook in boiling water for 5 minutes until tender. Drain well. Arrange a layer of aubergines in a large ovenproof dish, cover with tomato sauce then a layer of beans and Mozzarella cheese. Repeat the layers, finishing with aubergine. Sprinkle with the Parmesan cheese and breadcrumbs and cook in a preheated oven 190°C (375°F), gas mark 5 for 45 minutes until bubbling and crisp. Serve hot.

Note
Freezing is recommended for this recipe. Leave the Parmesan and breadcrumbs until defrosted and about to cook.

STUFFED FIELD MUSHROOMS WITH RED PESTO

Recipe sent by
Sarah Brown

Ingredients

Serves 2-4

4 large field mushrooms
2 tablespoons olive oil
2 cloves garlic, peeled and crushed
125 g (4 oz) pitted black olives
4 tablespoons chopped fresh basil
3-4 teaspoons Parmesan cheese

1 red pepper
1 onion, finely chopped
8 sun dried tomatoes (in oil)
2 teaspoons red pesto
salt and pepper

Method

Preheat the oven to 190°C (375°F) gas mark 5. Wipe or peel the mushrooms and remove the stalks. Chop the stalks finely and set aside. Wipe the red pepper and brush with a little oil. Bake for 40 minutes or until the skin is well charred. Leave to cool and then peel off the skin and remove the seeds. To make the filling, heat the remaining oil and fry the onion and garlic until soft, add the mushroom stalks and cook for 2-3 minutes. Put all the remaining ingredients, including the red pepper, into a food processor. Add the cooked onion mix and process until finely chopped. Season to taste and then pile onto the mushrooms. Place on an oiled shallow ovenproof tray and sprinkle a little Parmesan over each mushroom. Bake for 15 minutes. Serve hot.

Note

This is a good first course or part of a light meal. Red pesto adds colour but you can use green instead. The recipe is from 'Sarah Brown's Fresh Vegetarian Cookery' published by the BBC.

VEGETARIAN CHRISTMAS DISH

Recipe sent by
Dale Rapley

Ingredients
Serves 6

15ml (1 tablespoon) olive oil
1 large onion, chopped
2 sticks celery, chopped
2 cloves garlic, chopped
100 g (4 oz) mushrooms, finely chopped
170 g (6 oz) wholemeal breadcrumbs
100 g (4 oz) brazil nuts, chopped
50 g (2 oz) ground almonds
15 ml (1 tablespoon) wholegrain mustard
1 egg
450 g (1 lb) fresh leaf spinach
225 g (8 oz) curd cheese
2-5 ml (½ teaspoon) ground nutmeg
8 sheets filo pastry
50 g (2 oz) melted vegetarian margarine

Method
First fry the onion and celery until soft. Add the garlic and mushrooms
and cook for a further minute. Remove from the heat and stir in the
breadcrumbs, nuts, yeast extract and mustard. Season well and add the
egg to bind it together. Wash the spinach and place in a large bowl.
Cover with boiling water and leave for 1 minute to wilt, then drain,
pressing out the water. Mix the curd cheese and nutmeg. Preheat the
oven to 190°C (375°F) gas mark 5. Lay out a sheet of filo pastry
30 x 46 cm (12 x 18 inches) on a damp teatowel and brush with
margarine. Continue layering and brushing all the layers of filo pastry.

51

Place half the nut mixture down the centre, leaving 10 cm (4 inches) at each end to make ruffles. Place half the spinach on top, then the cheese mixture, then the remaining spinach and nut mixture. Bring both sides of the pastry up and over to enclose the filling. Press to seal. Place on a dampened baking sheet and brush with margarine. Bake for 30 minutes until well browned. Serve with vegetables or a green salad.

Note
Dale is a vegetarian and says that this is a tasty alternative to turkey at Christmas.

ROASTED VEGETABLES WITH HORSERADISH SAUCE

Recipe sent by
Louise Gold

Ingredients

Serves 2-4

350 g (12 oz) celeriac
350 g (12 oz) parsnips
350 g (12 oz) swede
350 g (12 oz) red onions
25 g (1 oz) butter
2 tablespoons olive oil
1 garlic bulb
lemon wedges (optional)

For the sauce
1-2 tablespoons horseradish relish
150 ml (5 fl oz) soured cream
or Greek yoghurt
salt and freshly ground black
pepper

Method

Set the oven to 200°C (400°F) gas mark 6. Put a large pan of water on the stove to heat. Peel the celeriac, parsnips and swede, then cut them into chunky pieces. Trim the tops off the onions and peel off the outer skin without removing the root. Cut into quarters, still leaving the root, which will hold them together. Put the butter and olive oil into a roasting tin and put into the oven to heat up. Meanwhile put the vegetables into the pan of water and boil for 5 minutes. Drain them, then put them into the sizzling hot fat and into the oven. Break the garlic into cloves. Add the unpeeled garlic to the vegetables after about 15 minutes, then continue roasting for a further 15-20 minutes or until they are golden brown. Serve at once, garnished with lemon wedges and accompanied by the sauce. To make the sauce, simply stir the horseradish relish into the soured cream or yoghurt and add seasoning to taste.

Note

Louise says that this recipe is easy to make and simply delicious! Roasting brings out the flavour of winter vegetables in a delightful way. They can be eaten as an accompanying vegetable or on their own as a complete course with the lemon juice squeezed over, a good sprinkling of coarse salt and the horseradish sauce. Leave out the garlic if you wish, but when cooked it becomes very mild and almost creamy.

The recipe is from Rose Elliot's *'Vegetarian Four Seasons'* published by Harper Collins.

PREET PALACE'S SAG CHANA (SPINACH AND CHICKPEA)

**Recipe sent by
Julie Christie**

Ingredients   Serves 4

400 g (14 oz) spinach, cooked, drained and chopped, or
   200 g frozen spinach, thawed and drained
225 g (8 oz) dried chickpeas, or a 425 g (15 oz) can
2 small potatoes, 200 g (3 oz)
1 teaspoon turmeric
4 tablespoons vegetable ghee or oil
1 tablespoon tomato purée
2 palmfuls fresh coriander
2 cm (¾ inch) fresh ginger, peeled and grated
2 garlic cloves, crushed
2 teaspoons salt
3 tablespoons green peppers, seeded and chopped
2½ tablespoons Balti spice mix
2 tomatoes, chopped
4/6 ladles Balti sauce

Basic Balti Sauce - Makes 750 ml (1½ pints)

3 tablespoons vegetable oil	½ teaspoon ground cumin
4 onions, chopped	½ teaspoon ground coriander
small piece ginger, peeled and grated	¼ teaspoon chilli powder
1 large garlic clove, crushed	salt to taste
1 tomato, chopped	palmful chopped fresh coriander
½ teaspoon turmeric	
1 teaspoon paprika	

Basic Balti Spice Mix (Makes 5 teaspoons)
2 teaspoons paprika
1½ teaspoons coriander
¾ teaspoon cumin
½ teaspoon salt
¼ teaspoon chilli powder or 1½ small dried red chillis

Method

Soak the chickpeas overnight then simmer for 1½ hours until tender and rain, OR open can and drain. Make the Balti sauce - heat the oil and fry the onion, ginger and garlic until translucent. Add the tomato and stir-fry, breaking it up with the spoon. Pour in 300 ml (½ pint) water and stir in the other ingredients. Cover and simmer 30 minutes. Cool then pour into blender or processor and liquidise. Boil the potatoes with the turmeric until nearly cooked. They should still be a little crisp inside when skewered. Drain and set aside. Heat the oil or ghee in a large wok. Put in the ginger, garlic and spinach. Stir well mashing up the spinach roughly. Add the salt and green peppers. Now add the potato pieces and as they cook, break them up. The spice mix is stirred in next, followed by the tomato purée, chickpeas, tomatoes, fresh coriander and 4 ladles Balti sauce. Shake the wok and stir vigorously, cooking for 3-4 minutes. Add more sauce if it is too dry. Divide among 4 warmed Balti dishes and serve with a Balti dip of yogurt and mint and poppadoms.

Note

Julie Christie makes this recipe as often as the yellow stained page in her book shows. It is from '*100 Best Balti Curries*' by Diane Lowe and Mike Davidson, who say it is simple enough for an indulgent one person supper but interesting enough for a dinner party.

MRS BAZELY'S KURAMA

Recipe sent by
Paul Bazely

Ingredients   Serves 4

This curry can be made with meat or vegetables.
450g (1 lb) any preferred meat or a variety of vegetables
2 onions, chopped
1 teaspoon chilli powder
1 teaspoon ginger paste or fresh ginger, grated
1 teaspoon garlic paste or chopped cloves
1 teaspoon turmeric
2-3 teaspoons coriander paste or 1 bunch fresh leaves, chopped
1 - 2 tablespoons oil
1 inch piece creamed coconut
salt to taste

Method

Cube the meat or dice the vegetables. Fry the onion in oil until tender.
Add the chilli, ginger, garlic and turmeric and fry well until the oil rises
to the surface. Add a little water if the mixture gets too dry. Then add
the meat or vegetables and fry again. Lastly add the coriander, salt and
coconut and enough water to cover. Cook until tender and sauce is
thickened. Serve hot with Pilau Rice or Bhatura (fried puffed whole
wheat bread).

Note

This curry recipe is Paul's Mother's traditional recipe.

PILAU RICE

Recipe sent by
Paul Bazely

Ingredients
approximately ½ cup Basmati rice per person
2 onions, chopped
2 sticks cinnamon
4 cloves
3 to 4 cardamom pods
2 to 3 cloves garlic, crushed
salt to taste
2 tablespoons oil

Method
Wash the rice 3 or 4 times to prevent sticking. Fry the onions, cinnamon, cloves, cardamoms and garlic in the oil. Add rice and 2 cups water per cup of rice if cooked in the oven or a cup of water per cup of rice if cooked on the hob. Seal the pan with a firm lid. Cook on the hob over a low heat for 15 to 20 minutes or in the oven on 190°C (375°F) gas mark 5 for about 20 minutes. Keep checking to ensure it does not dry out. When cooked remove and serve hot.

TORTILLA (SPANISH OMELETTE)

Recipe sent by
Sally Ann Triplett

Ingredients   Serves 4
1 large onion
4 medium potatoes
8 large eggs
olive oil

Method
Peel and dice the onion. Put a little olive oil in a non-stick frying pan
and heat on a low setting. Add the onion and slowly soften until it starts
to turn golden brown but not crispy. Peel and thinly slice the potatoes.
In a second pan heat more oil or use the same pan and remove the
onions. Add the sliced potatoes and salt, cover with a lid or plate and
cook gently, turning the slices frequently until soft. Add the onions and
mix without breaking the potato slices. Beat the eggs in a bowl large
enough to hold the potatoes and onion as well. Season, then add the
potato and onion mixture and leave to stand for 5 minutes. The egg
should cover all the mixture. Put the whole mixture into the frying pan,
cover and cook on a very low heat for about 20 minutes, turning once
or twice. Serve with sliced Spanish tomatoes.

Note
At college we were always told to 'think thin'. Our lunch, consisting of
two ryvitas, tab of butter, chunk of cheese and apple, was hardly enough
to feed a fly. So when breaktime came around, late afternoon, we would
take ourselves off to the Italian Café around the corner where Sophie
would always say what everyone else was thinking - "I want something
really big." We were, of course, all famished and would hastily indulge

in fat sandwiches, cakes and frothy cappuccinos, by which time it was only possible to 'think fat'. My memories of college days are some of the happiest of my life, mostly due to my friendship with Sophie. I shall always miss her.

TIM FLAVIN'S 'RIB STICKIN' GOOD' SCALLOPED POTATOES

Recipe sent by
Tim Flavin
Serves 4-6

Ingredients

700 g (1½ lbs potatoes)
1½ cups milk
2 tablespoons butter
1 teaspoon salt

fresh ground pepper to taste
1 clove garlic, pressed
1 large chopped leek
1 cup grated cheese

Method

Preheat the oven to 180°C (350°F) gas mark 4. Wash and pare the potatoes and cut into thick slices lengthwise. Combine all the ingredients except the cheese in a saucepan. Bring to the boil and simmer 15 minutes, stirring often. Transfer to a well greased baking dish. Sprinkle with the cheese. Be liberal. Bake in a preheated oven about 30 minutes or until the potatoes are tender and the cheese is bubbly and brown.

Note

Serve as a side dish with chops, steak, fish, chicken, any ol' thing and complement with a green salad. "Rib Stickin' good!" says Tim!

ROBIN'S RISOTTO

Recipe sent by
Colin Sell

Ingredients   Serves 2

1 onion
100 - 125 g (4 - 5 oz) rice
herbs of your choice
parsley, chopped
a few drops balsamic vinegar
½ glass white wine
salt and pepper
1 red pepper

Method

Finely chop the onion and cut the pepper into strips. Boil the rice until cooked, then drain. Fry the onion gently in 2 tablespoons olive oil. Season well and add the herbs and red pepper strips. Fry gently for a few minutes longer. Add the chopped parsley and a few drops of balsamic vinegar. Stir in the wine and allow to bubble then add the rice. Stir and serve. Leave the washing up until next morning!

Note

While not a conventional risotto this recipe is one of the first created by Colin Sell's son when he was eight years old (now nine). It incorporates two of the most important principles of improvisational cooking:
1. When you don't know what to cook start by frying an onion.
2. Most things are improved by adding some wine.

PASTA

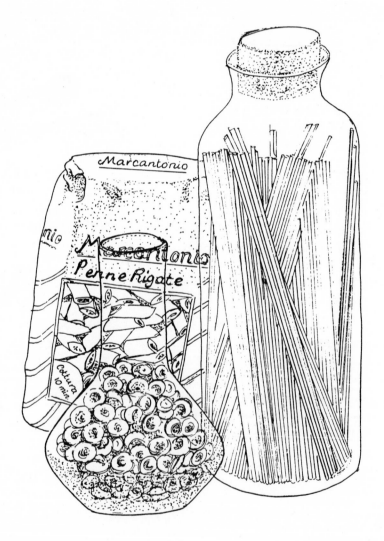

SPINACH PASTA

Recipe sent by
Michael French

Ingredients

Serves 8

75 - 100 g (3 - 4 oz) pasta per person
4 garlic cloves, halved
100 g (4 oz) shelled pistachio nuts
400 g (14 oz) Gorgonzola cheese
8 tablespoons milk
8 tablespoons double cream
8 tablespoons Parmesan cheese
1 handful of chopped flat leaf parsley
salt and pepper
6 handfuls fresh spinach

Method

Cook the pasta (such as penne, rigatoni) as directed. Cook the spinach for a few minutes and drain well. Grate the Parmesan cheese and crumble the Gorgonzola. Melt the butter in a saucepan, add the garlic, cloves and nuts and cook for a few minutes. Remove the garlic with a slotted spoon and add the Gorgonzola and milk. When the cheese has melted and the sauce is creamy, remove from the heat and stir in the cream. Reheat gently without boiling. Toss the sauce with the pasta, spinach, Parmesan and parsley. Season well. Place on the table in a very large, heated serving dish and let everyone help themselves! Accompany with lots of garlic bread, a huge bowl of salad and plenty of good wine.

Note

This is one of the dishes Michael rustles up when he has friends to a meal at short notice. It is quick and tasty and perfect for long evenings with good wine and conversation.

THIS PAGE
SPONSORED BY
LORD & LADY PUTTNAM

SOPHIE'S CHOICE

Recipe sent by
Stifyn Parri and Charles Shirvell

Ingredients
Serves 2

penne pasta - enough for 2 people
55 g (2 oz) Dolcelatte cheese
55 g (2 oz) broken walnuts
2 dessertspoons pesto sauce
½ small carton sour cream
salt and freshly ground black pepper
a palmful of shaved Parmesan cheese

Method
Put a serving dish and plates to warm. Boil the pasta until firm but cooked ('al dente'). Whilst you are waiting, cut the cheese into small pieces. Drain the pasta and return to the same hot pan. Add the Dolcelatte, walnuts, pesto sauce and sour cream. Stir altogether and serve immediately. Sprinkle with the Parmesan shavings.

Note
Sophie used to love eating this pasta dish whenever she came for supper. The recipe is so simple and adaptable. You can use a different cheese or nuts or even cooked ham or bacon. Wash down with a large glass of wine!

JOAN'S PERFECT PASTA

Recipe sent by
Andrew Hesker

Ingredients   Serves 4

1 large courgette
2 red peppers
100 g (4 oz) button mushrooms
350 g (12 oz) pasta quills
2 tablespoons olive oil
1 onion, peeled and finely chopped
2 cloves garlic, peeled and crushed
50 g (2 oz) frozen peas
salt and freshly ground black pepper
1 tablespoon chives, snipped
1 tablespoon olive oil
50 g (2 oz) grated Cheddar cheese

Method

Trim the courgettes and slice thinly lengthways, then chop slices into
lengths. Seed the peppers and slice into strips. Slice the mushrooms.
Cook the pasta in slightly salted boiling water for 12 minutes or until
tender. Drain and place in a large bowl, cover and keep warm. Heat the
oil in a pan and fry the onion and garlic until soft but not brown.
Remove with a slotted spoon and reserve. Add the courgette, peppers
and mushrooms and cook until softened. Return the onion and garlic
and add the peas. Season and heat through. Pour over the hot pasta, add
the chives and drizzle over the olive oil. Toss to mix. Arrange on
heatproof plates and sprinkle with the cheese. Place under a preheated
grill until golden.

Note

Andy says: "During our many years of friendship, Soph and I had dinner many, many times and were constantly on the lookout for slimming/low fat recipes - and as I love pasta, when we discovered this particular recipe it seemed ideal. It also had terrific camp value as we found it in the TV Times *'Cook with the Stars'* booklet, a recipe submitted by Joan Collins. It made me laugh!"
(Copyright Pisces Worldwide Ltd.)

KATE'S 5 MINUTE SUMMER SALAD

**Recipe sent by
Kate Valentine**

Ingredients

Serves 4-6

1 pack spinach and ricotta Tortellini
1 pack washed and trimmed watercress
1 large pack broccoli florets
4 courgettes
1 large carton cottage cheese

Method

Parboil the broccoli. Pan fry the courgettes in olive oil and rosemary. Boil the pasta until 'al dente'. Combine the broccoli, courgettes, cottage cheese and pasta with the watercress in a large salad bowl. Toss well and add salt and pepper to taste. Serve still warm with tomato salad and crusty bread.

PASTA PRIMAVERA

Recipe sent by
Joan Collins

Ingredients   Serves 6
500 g (1 lb) penne
1 broccoli head
2 medium sized courgettes
2 medium sized onions
8 large mushrooms
2 large tomatoes
2 cloves garlic
grated Parmesan cheese (optional)
a little butter

Method
Cook the pasta in boiling water for 12 minutes (until al dente). Drain and refresh with boiling water (removing excess starch). Break the broccoli head into florets and steam for 7 minutes until cooked but still crunchy. Chop the onions coarsely and sauté in butter until soft. (If you have a microwave put the onions in a bowl with ½ inch water, cover with clingfilm and cook for 2½ minutes. Drain.) Add the onions to the pasta. Wash the courgettes and cut into 2 inch strips. Steam for about 5 minutes until cooked. Clean the mushrooms with salt and kitchen paper or peel them. Place under a hot grill for a few minutes. Drain on kitchen paper then cut into chunks. Concasse the tomatoes by placing in boiling water for 10 seconds. Remove the skins, quarter, then cut each in half again. Remove the seeds. Crush the garlic and add to the vegetables. Season with salt and pepper. Add the vegetables, except the broccoli, to the pasta and reheat gently.
Reheat the broccoli in the steamer then add carefully to the pasta. Add

Parmesan for more flavour but this is not essential. Serve warm, not too hot. It's scrumptious and a healthy dish that children will savour.

Note

This is one of Joan Collins' favourite recipes for pasta. Once spurned by dieters, there has been a rethink on pasta and it is now recognised as an excellent source of carbohydrates and a perfect energy food. Choose wholewheat pasta as it contains fibre and serve with a light tomato and herb sauce, but do not be tempted into topping it with a rich cream sauce high in calories.

ITALIAN PASTA BAKE

Recipe sent by
Pauline Quirke and Linda Robson

Ingredients   Serves 4

225 g (8 oz) penne pasta
salt and pepper
275 g (10 oz) ham, cut into strips
butter for greasing
3 eggs
450 ml (1 pint) single cream
150 g (5 oz) Gruyère cheese, grated
50 g (2 oz) Parmesan cheese, grated

Method
Preheat the oven to 190°C (375°F) gas mark 5. Put the pasta in a pan of boiling salted water and cook for 8-10 minutes until just tender. Drain well. Stir the ham into the pasta and put into a greased ovenproof dish. Beat together the eggs, cream and seasoning and add half the Gruyère cheese. Pour over the pasta. Sprinkle the remaining Gruyère and the Parmesan over the top and bake for 40 minutes until golden.

Note
Whatever kind of pasta you use, always allow 50 - 75 g (2 - 3 oz) per person.

THIS PAGE
SPONSORED BY
ALEC McCOWEN

PASTA TWIRLS

**Recipe sent by
Amanda Redman**

Ingredients   Serves 4

75 - 110 g (3 - 4 oz) per person, pasta twirls
5 rashers bacon, grilled and chopped
12 potatoes, boiled
1 onion, sliced and fried
Cheddar cheese, grated
oil for frying

Method

Peel and chop the onion, grill the bacon rashers and boil the potatoes. Fry the onion until soft then add the sliced potatoes and grilled bacon, chopped. Sauté until potatoes are browned. Meanwhile cook the pasta. When the mixture in the frying pan is ready, sprinkle with grated cheese and brown under the grill. Serve the mixture on top of the pasta. Add oodles of tomato sauce.

BOLOGNESE SAUCE

Recipe sent by
Barbara Jefford OBE

Ingredients   Serves 5-6

500 g (1 lb) minced beef   2 tablespoons tomato purée
225 g (8 oz) streaky bacon, chopped   570 ml (1 pint) beef stock
1 large onion, roughly chopped   2 bay leaves
4/5 sticks celery, roughly chopped   Worcestershire sauce
340 g (12 oz) mushrooms, roughly chopped
3 tablespoons olive oil   1 large glass red wine
400 g (14 oz) can/700 g (1½ lb) peeled tomatoes
garlic salt, black pepper, Italian seasoning or mixed herbs

Method

Fry the onion, celery and bacon in 1½ tablespoons oil until soft. Heat
the remaining oil in a saucepan and when smoking add the mince and
cook until brown. Add the onion, celery and bacon and cook on a low
to medium heat. Add the stock, mushrooms, tomatoes, purée, a good
sprinkling of herbs and seasonings and a few drops of Worcestershire
sauce. Turn up the heat, cook briskly, stirring for about 5 minutes then
turn the heat down and simmer for about ¾ hour until the sauce is
pourable but thick. Just before serving stir in the wine and pour over
the cooked pasta. Sprinkle with grated Parmesan cheese and serve.

Note

Barbara Jefford says this will do for two people since, if the sauce is kept
in the refrigerator it may be microwaved two or three times: very
convenient for after-the-theatre suppers. She has been using the recipe
for at least 40 years and it came originally from an Australian friend.

PASTA WITH CHEESE AND WALNUT SAUCE

Recipe sent by
Nicholas Hytner

Ingredients   Serves 4

455 g (1 lb) large pasta, such as penne or shells
225 g (8 oz) cream cheese - Mascarpone or a mixture of Mascarpone and
    creamy blue such as Gorgonzola
100 g (4 oz) chopped walnuts
butter
Parmesan cheese

Method

Cook the pasta in boiling water. Meanwhile melt a large lump of butter
in a saucepan and stir in the cheese. Heat but don't boil. Then stir in
the cooked pasta, walnuts and a generous amount of Parmesan cheese.

Note

Nicholas Hytner recommends that as this is a politically incorrect recipe
you could eat it with an undressed tomato salad to feel virtuous. It is
unbelievably quick and easy and comforting after a difficult late night
rehearsal.

MEAT
AND
POULTRY

STAYABED STEW

Recipe sent by
Dorothy Tutin
Serves 5-6

Ingredients

1 kilo (2 lbs) stewing beef, cubed
1 tin little tiny peas *
1 cup sliced carrots
2 sliced onions
½ teaspoon salt, dash of pepper
1 tin cream of tomato soup (thinned with ½ tin water)
  or celery or mushroom soup, thinned likewise
1 big raw potato, sliced
a bay leaf *

* if you don't like this leave it out

Method

Preheat the oven to 140°C (275°F) gas mark 1. Mix everything up and put it in a casserole dish with a tight lid. Put the lid on and put the casserole in the oven. Now go back to bed. It will cook happily by itself and be done in 5 hours.

Note

Dorothy Tutin says this is for those days when you're *en negligée,* with a murder story and a box of chocolates or possibly a good case of 'flu. It is so easy and really works and is marvellous when you're busy.

HUGH'S HOT POT

Recipe sent by
Hugh Lloyd

Ingredients   Serves 4-6

1 kilo (1¾ lbs) lean chuck steak
6 medium potatoes
5 sticks celery
4 medium onions
a beef stock cube
1 tablespoon flour
salt and black pepper
25 g (1 oz) butter

Method

First, keep the wife out of the kitchen! Preheat the oven to 170°C
(350°F) gas mark 3. Then cut the steak into 2½ cm (1 inch) cubes and
toss them in seasoned flour. Peel and slice the potatoes - not too thinly.
Chop the celery into 5 cm (2 inch) pieces. Peel and slice the onions. Put
half the meat into a large casserole pot, cover with half the celery, half
the onions and half the potatoes. Season lightly. Repeat the procedure
with the remaining ingredients and dot the top layer of potatoes with
butter and season. Make up the stock cube with 1 pint of boiling water
and pour over the ingredients. Cover the casserole with a lid and cook
for at least 2 hours. Then remove the lid and continue cooking for a
further 30 minutes until the potatoes are brown.

Note

"This should last about three days - and gets better day by day!" says
Hugh Lloyd.

MOVIE STEW

Recipe sent by
Janet Suzman

Ingredients

Serves any number

Take whatever you find in the fridge - leftover celery, carrots,
 parsnips, etc
1 onion
200 g (½ lb) per person good quality stewing beef, pork or lamb
1 tin Heinz tomato soup (this is the secret weapon)
1 tin red beans, including the juice
1 chilli pepper
a spoon or two of concentrated tomato purée
a little stock

Method

Remove the fat from the meat and cut into bite-size pieces. Chop the
onion and chilli and cut the vegetables where necessary. Chuck
everything into the heavy saucepan. Mix the soup, tomato purée and
stock and pour it in. Put the lid on and simmer for a few hours on a low
heat. Voilà! The secret is no fat and no pre-sealing of anything. Serve
with baked potatoes or rice and green salad.

Note

This is Janet Suzman's standby recipe for sudden influxes of people, so
named because you can put it on, go to the movies and it's ready when
you return.

CHILLI CON CARNE

Recipe sent by
Wendy Richard

Ingredients   Serves 6-8

1.35 kg (3 lbs) lean mince   3 chicken bouillon cubes
Schwartz chilli essence to taste   450 g (1 lb) onions, chopped
450 g (1 lb) mushrooms, chopped   4 garlic cloves
1 tin red sweet pimentos
½ bar Meuniers cooking chocolate - green wrapper
¼ bottle tarragon vinegar   3 tablespoons brown sugar
1 tablespoon cumin   1 tablespoon coriander
1 tablespoon oregano   3 tins red kidney beans
3 tins tomatoes   tomato paste

Method
Fry the onions in a little olive oil with the crushed garlic. Add the meat
together with all the seasonings. Add the rest of the vegetables then mix
the chicken stock with water and pour it over. There should be enough
just to cover the ingredients. Then add the chocolate and the tomato
paste. Gently simmer for about 3 hours, stirring occasionally. Serve
with rice or pasta. Grated cheese is also a good addition if sprinkled over
the top of each portion.

Note
This dish freezes well and gains strength in flavour.

DELICIOUS PORK CHOPS

Recipe sent by
Julia McKenzie
Serves 2

Ingredients
2 loin pork chops
25 g (1 oz) butter
fresh or dried sage or oregano
1 onion, chopped
1 apple, sliced and chopped
2 tablespoons double cream
salt and pepper
2 large pieces of foil

Method
Preheat the oven to180°C (350°F) gas mark 4. Cut 2 large pieces of foil
and lightly oil them. Gently sauté the chops in the butter on both sides
until golden. Place one on each piece of foil. Season and rub with sage
or oregano. Fry the chopped onions and apples briefly in the same pan
and cover the chops with the mixture. Pour 1 tablespoon of cream over
the top of each. Bring the edges of foil together loosely and crimp the
edges. Place on a baking tray in the oven for 45 minutes to 1 hour.
Delicious! Serve with new potatoes and a green salad.

Note
This is Julia McKenzie's adaptation of a Carrier recipe and is a fast
favourite.

GREEK LAMB

Recipe sent by
Michelle Newell
Serves 4

Ingredients
½ leg lamb (bone in)
6 cloves garlic, unpeeled
1½ tablespoons olive oil
juice of 1 lemon
small wineglass of water
salt and pepper

Method
Preheat the oven to 150°C (300°F) gas mark 2. Heat the oil in a heavy-bottomed, lidded, cast iron casserole dish or roasting dish and kitchen foil. Brown the lamb on all sides. Season liberally with salt and freshly ground black pepper, add the lemon juice, water and garlic cloves. Tightly cover with close-fitting lid or foil and put in the oven for approximately 3 hours. Walk away and enjoy a glass of wine or do the school pick-up. After 1½ hours turn the meat over and baste with the cooking juices. Replace the lid or foil so that no steam escapes. Check towards the end that the meat is tender - it is best when practically falling off the bone. Take out of the oven and leave to rest, covered, for a few minutes to make carving easier. (It does not cut elegantly but perhaps that is a small price to pay for tenderness and flavour.) Serve with the cooking juices spooned over (and cooked garlic pressed out of the skins if liked). Accompany with a Greek salad, boiled Basmati rice and the rest of the bottle of wine you opened earlier!

Note

This, says Michelle Newell, is a well-tempered, slow-braised dish that allows you a life! Michelle's recipes have evolved over many years of enjoying cooking and as she is an old-fashioned cook, she never measures or times anything so hopes they are accurate enough for other people to follow, but, most of all, to enjoy.

GREEK SALAD TO ACCOMPANY THE LAMB

Ingredients   Serves 4

175 g (6 oz) Feta cheese, cut into small cubes
6 ripe tomatoes, quartered
½ cucumber, cut into chunks
½ red onion, thinly sliced
50 g (2 oz) black olives, preferably stoned
4 tablespoons olive oil
a little lemon juice
salt and freshly milled black pepper
lemon wedges to garnish

Method

Mix the cheese, tomatoes, cucumber, olives and onion lightly together in a salad bowl. Mix the olive oil with a little lemon juice and the seasoning and pour over the salad. Garnish with lemon wedges.

LAMB WITH ORANGE AND RED WINE

Recipe sent by
Richard Cawley

Ingredients

Serves 6

3 tablespoons olive oil

900 g (2 lbs) lamb neck fillet, cubed

2 large onions, coarsely chopped

5 cloves garlic, roughly chopped

75 g (3 oz) pitted black olives

juice and grated zest of 1 small orange

1 bottle red wine

1 sprig rosemary

1 bay leaf

salt and pepper

2-3 sprigs fresh thyme

Orange gremolata

3 heaped tablespoons flat leafed parsley

2 cloves garlic, chopped

the finely pared zest of 1 small orange cut into 'splinters'

Method

Preheat the oven to 350°C (180°F) gas mark 4. Heat the oil in a large saucepan or lidded casserole and fry the meat in batches until seared and browned. Remove with a slotted spoon and set aside. Add the onions and stir fry until softened but not browned - about 10 minutes. Add the garlic, olives, bay leaf, orange juice and rind, herbs, salt and pepper and the wine. Bring to the boil, stirring well. Return the meat and if the liquid does not cover it, top up with water. Cover the pan tightly, using foil as well if the lid isn't a perfect fit. Cook undisturbed in the oven for 3 hours or until the meat is tender. Serve in warmed-up soup dishes sprinkled with a little of the orange gremolata.

Note

Richard Cawley says "This is a delicious, simple but heart-warming casserole, with more than a hint of the Mediterranean, suitable for entertaining or just a splendid midweek family meal."

DUCK LEGS BRAISED WITH GINGER, CINNAMON AND CHILLIS

**Recipe sent by
Kerry Fox**

Ingredients
Serves 6

6 large duck legs, trimmed of excess fat, with foot and ankle removed

¾ cup coarsely grated fresh ginger   2 carrots cut into 1 cm dice

3 red onions, peeled and quartered   6 cloves garlic, peeled and
                                                                    crushed

2 cinnamon quills   3 red chillis sliced into rings with seeds intact

1 tablespoon Nam Pla (Asian fish sauce)

1 tablespoon tamari or soy sauce

Method

Preheat the oven to 220°C (425°F) gas mark 7. Put all the ingredients except the legs into a deep casserole dish or roasting pan and mix well. Lay the legs on top but don't overlap them. Pour on enough boiling water to almost cover the legs then seal the dish tightly with a lid or foil. Place in the oven and cook for 2½ hours, remove the lid and continue to cook until the legs are brown and crispy. Taste for seasoning then serve, ideally with boiled rice or sweet potatoes and lots of fresh coriander.

Note

This recipe is a creation of Kerry's friend Peter. Peter is head chef at the Sugar Club Restaurant in Notting Hill. Kerry and Peter are from New Zealand and the dish has an obvious Asian/Pacific quality. Peter says the dish reminds him a lot of the stews he ate in Malaysia and Thailand when backpacking through Asia in the mid-80's. Once the ingredients are assembled and in the oven you can leave it to look after itself.

DUCK IN ORANGE, ROSEMARY AND WHITE WINE

Recipe sent by
Ben Kingsley

Recipe   Serves 2

1 boneless duck breast per person
1 tablespoon flour
seasoning
olive oil or good chicken fat for browning
½ glass orange juice
½ glass dry white wine
2 sprigs rosemary
1 cupful sloe berries (if available)

Method

Coat the duck breasts in seasoned flour. Heat the olive oil or chicken fat
and quickly brown both sides in it. When the meat is sealed add ½ glass
orange juice, ½ glass white wine and the rosemary. Ben Kingsley adds
a cupful of sloe berries from his sloe gin as well. Reduce the heat and
simmer gently for about ½ hour or until the meat is very tender.
Remove the breasts, slice and arrange on a heated dish and keep in a
warm place. Meanwhile reduce the liquid over a high heat, pour over
the sliced duck and serve to loud applause!

Note

Ben Kingsley recommends serving the duck with new potatoes and
courgettes, thinly sliced and fried with spring onions.

SPICY CHICKEN CHILLI
(It cooks itself)

Recipe sent by
Debra Stables

Ingredients   Serves 4

4 large or 6 smaller chicken thighs on the bone (skin removed)
1 medium red pepper   1 medium green pepper
1 large onion or 6 shallots
200 g (8 oz) mushrooms (closed cup or shitake)
2 large carrots   2 medium courgettes
4 cloves garlic   1 x 380 g (14 oz) tin chilli beans (in sauce)
1 tablespoon tomato purée   ½ cup water or dry white wine
1 crumbled chicken stock cube   1 teaspoon ground cumin
1 teaspoon ground coriander   1 teaspoon mild chilli powder
salt and pepper to taste

Method
Preheat the oven to 180°C (350°F) gas mark 4. Chop all the vegetables quite chunkily. Mix all the vegetables together in a large casserole, placing the chicken thighs on top. Mix the stock cube, wine, cumin, coriander, chilli powder, seasoning and tomato purée and pour over the casserole. Cover with a lid and put into the oven for 1 hour. Remove the lid and cook for a further 15-20 minutes uncovered. Taste for seasoning and serve with baked or mashed potatoes or rice.

Note
This is Debra's friend John's recipe which he cooked for her when he visited Toronto recently.

TWO MINUTE CHICKEN

Recipe sent by
Sir Cameron Mackintosh

Ingredients   Serves 2
2 chicken breasts
a handful chopped coriander
1 cm (½ inch) fresh ginger, thinly sliced into slivers
good olive oil - enough to coat
2 teaspoons fresh pesto
a squeeze of lemon juice
salt and pepper

Method
Slice each breast into thin wafers, between ½ and ¼ inch. Place in a dish
and marinate with freshly chopped coriander, slivers of ginger, olive oil,
pesto and lemon juice, salt and pepper. Leave in the fridge for at least a
couple of hours. When ready to eat, lightly oil a griddle pan and when
hot, cook the chicken, turning regularly to stop it sticking - about one
minute each side should be sufficient. Serve immediately.

Note
Serve with a mixed green salad or boiled new potatoes and batons of
courgettes and an assortment of lightly sautéed mushrooms - truffle oil
is delicious if you have it!

CHICKEN CACCIATORA
Pollo alla Cacciatora

Recipe sent by
Michael Pennington

Ingredients

Serves 4-6

1 chicken 1.5 - 2 kg (3 - 4 lbs) at room temperature, cut into 8 serving
  pieces
sea salt and freshly ground black pepper
3 tablespoons extra virgin olive oil
1 tablespoon unsalted butter
1 small onion, minced
2 ribs celery, thinly sliced
¼ teaspoon crushed red peppers (hot red pepper flakes)
1 x 765 g (28 oz) can peeled Italian plum tomatoes in juice or crushed
  tomatoes in purée
several sprigs fresh parsley, bay leaves, fresh rosemary and celery leaves,
  tied in a bundle with cotton thread

Method

Season the chicken pieces liberally with salt and pepper. In a large frying
pan combine the oil and butter over a high heat. Add several pieces of
chicken and cook skin side down until an even golden brown, about 5
minutes. Turn and brown them on the other side, about 5 minutes
more. Do not crowd the pan. Brown the chicken in several batches.
Avoid scorching the skin. When browned transfer to a platter. Add the
onion, celery, crushed red peppers and salt to the fat in the pan and cook
over a moderate heat until soft and translucent for 4 or 5 minutes. If
using whole tomatoes purée them in a food mill straight into the pan.
The crushed tomatoes can be added straight from the can. Add the herb

86

bundle, stir to blend and simmer for 5 minutes. Bury the chicken in the sauce and simmer, partly covered, until cooked through 25 to 30 minutes more. Remove herb bundle and discard. Transfer the chicken to warmed dinner plates, along with the sauce. Serve immediately on its own or with steamed or boiled potatoes.

Note

This is the best Cacciatora Michael Pennington knows and he says the secret is plenty of tomatoes and the celery. The recipe is from Patricia Wells' book *'Trattoria; An Italian Celebration'*, published by Kyle Cathie Ltd, 1993. Patricia Wells says 'Be sure to buy the best chicken you can find; it will make all the difference between an everyday dish and one that's really special.'

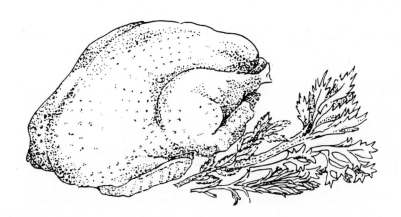

CHICKEN AND NUT CASSEROLE

Recipe sent by
Kathy Staff

Ingredients

Serves 4

4 chicken breasts
100 g (4 oz) mixed vegetables
100 g (4 oz) mushrooms
1 tin tomatoes
2 tablespoons white wine
4 tablespoons double cream
sliced almonds

Method

Preheat the oven to 200°C (400°F) gas mark 6. Put the sliced vegetables, mushrooms and tomatoes into an ovenproof dish. Lay the chicken pieces on top and season well. Cook, covered, for 1½ hours. Before serving, pour a tablespoon of cream over each chicken breast and sprinkle with nuts.

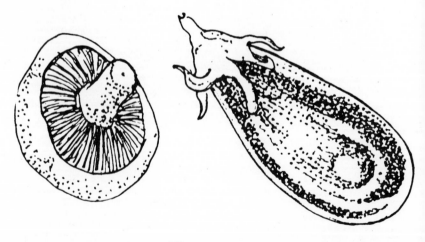

CHICKEN, CASHEW NUT AND VEGETABLE COUSCOUS

**Recipe sent by
Simon Cryer**

Ingredients
Serves 2-4

100 g (4 oz) cashew nuts
3 tablespoons soy sauce
6 tablespoons olive oil
2 cloves garlic, crushed
1 teaspoon curry powder
3 tablespoons tomato purée
1 vegetable stock cube
350 ml (12 fl oz) water
2 chicken breasts, cooked and diced
salt and freshly ground black pepper

1 onion, chopped
225 g (8 oz) sliced courgettes
1 green pepper, diced
225 g (8 oz) couscous
225 g (8 oz) sliced mushrooms
40 ml (2 fl oz) white wine or
   white wine vinegar
fresh herbs as required

Method

Preheat the oven to 190°C (375°F) gas mark 5. Roast the cashew nuts until brown then remove from oven and coat with soy sauce. Heat the oil in a large pan and gently fry the onion, then add the curry powder, garlic and tomato purée. Make up the vegetable stock with the water and add it to the pan, then add the courgettes, green pepper and chicken. Simmer for 2 minutes. Add the couscous, remove from the heat, cover and set aside. Meanwhile cook the mushrooms in a little olive oil, then add them to the mixture along with the cashew nuts. Add the white wine and season. Serve hot or cold.

PUDDINGS
AND
CAKES

VANILLA APPLE CAKE

Recipe sent by
Sybil Blackburn

Ingredients   Serves 4-6
100 g (4 oz) butter
100 g (4 oz) castor sugar
2 eggs, beaten
200 g (8 oz) self-raising four
1 large, thinly sliced apple
a little milk
½ teaspoon vanilla essence

Method
Preheat the oven to 170°C (325°F) gas mark 3. Well grease a cake tin.
Cream the butter and sugar together until soft and fluffy. Add the
beaten egg and vanilla a little at a time and beat well. Fold in the sieved
flour then the sliced apple, using a little milk if necessary. Bake until it
springs up when you gently press the top, for about 30-40 minutes.

Note
This is Sybil Blackburn's recipe from the early 1960's and is delicious
with creamy custard or fresh cream.

MARY'S OLD FASHIONED TREACLE TART

Recipe sent by
Sir Alan Ayckbourn

Ingredients
Serves 4-6

Pastry

Filling

150 g (6 oz) plain flour

225 g (8 oz) golden syrup

50 g (2 oz) margarine

40 g (1½ oz) fresh white breadcrumbs

25 g (1 oz) lard

finely grated rind of 1 lemon

1 egg yolk

beaten egg to glaze

cold water (enough to form a stiff dough)

Method

Preheat the oven to 190°C (375°F) gas mark 5. You will need a 20 cm (8 inch) fluted flan tin. Make the pastry using the short crust method. Roll it into a circle, line the flan tin and reserve the trimmings*, then chill for 30 minutes. To make the filling, warm the syrup in a saucepan with the lemon rind and juice (do not boil). Then mix in the breadcrumbs. Pour into the chilled flan case. Make strips from the reserved trimmings* and place these over the tart in a lattice pattern. Brush with a little beaten egg. Bake for 25 minutes or until the filling is just set. Serve with a custard sauce.

Microwave tip

Put the syrup in a basin and microwave on full power for 1-1½ minutes, then mix in the lemon rind, juice and breadcrumbs.

Note

This is Sir Alan's housekeeper, Mary Vardy's recipe for treacle tart - certainly the best he has ever eaten. "I suspect it is largely to do with her wonderful light hand with the pastry and, of course, that knack is impossible to impart."

MILLIE DAVIDSON'S CHEESE CAKE

Recipe sent by
Wendy Richard

Ingredients
560 g (1¼ lb) curd cheese
225 g (8 oz) castor sugar
pinch of salt
½ teaspoon vanilla essence
3 large eggs
2 tablespoons double cream
1 tablespoon sifted cornflour
digestive biscuits

Method
Butter a 23 cm (9 inch) loose bottomed tin. Preheat the oven to 180°C
(350°F) gas mark 4. Crush the digestive biscuits and sprinkle the bottom
of the tin with some of them. Beat the cheese well, add the salt, vanilla
essence and sugar and beat again. Beat in each egg, add the cream and
fold in the cornflour. Pour over the base and sprinkle the top with a few
biscuits. Bake for 35 minutes then switch off the oven and leave for a
further 35 minutes without opening the oven door. This dish freezes
well.

Note
Millie Davidson was a Jewish widow who lived in the same block of flats
as Wendy Richard. She told Wendy that for years she and her husband
had a cream cheese factory in the East End of London. They made only
the finest cream cheese.

GOLDEN LEMON MERINGUE PIE

**Recipe sent by
Ainsley Harriott**

Ingredients
Serves 4

grated rind and juice of 2 lemons
1 teaspoon cornflour
2 eggs
50 g (2 oz) unsalted butter, diced
175 g (6 oz) caster sugar
200 g (7 oz) shortcrust pastry
For the meringue
25 g (8 oz) granulated sugar
3 egg whites
½ teaspoon salt
few drops vanilla essence

Method
Preheat the oven to 200°C (400°F) gas mark 6. Make the meringue;
place the sugar in a small pan with 4 tablespoons of water and gently
bring to the boil, stirring until the sugar dissolves. Boil rapidly without
stirring for 3-4 minutes until the mixture turns pale golden. Roll out the
pastry on a floured surface and line four 12 cm (5 inch) tartlet tins. Prick
the bases, line with greaseproof paper and fill with baking beans. Bake
for 8 minutes, remove the beans and cook a further 6-7 minutes until
golden brown. Place the lemon rind, juice, cornflour, eggs, butter and
caster sugar in a small pan. Heat gently, stirring until the butter melts.
Bring the mixture to the boil and cook for 1-2 minutes until smooth and
thickened. Transfer to a bowl and leave to cool. Place the egg whites
and salt in a large glass bowl and whisk until the mixture forms soft
peaks. Pour in the hot syrup in a slow, steady stream, whisking

94

continuously to make stiff, glossy meringue. Remove the pastry cases from the oven and pour in the lemon filling. Spoon the meringue into a piping bag and pipe the meringue in a spiral on top of the lemon filling. Place the pies under a preheated grill for 1-2 minutes until the top is tinged with brown.

Note
Ainsley recommends serving the pie with lashings of cream!

EMERGENCY DESSERT

**Recipe sent by
Belinda Lang**

Ingredients   Serves 4
1 litre (1¾ pints) very creamy yoghurt
3 or 4 spoons of good marmalade
a good sprinkling of ginger

Method
Mix everything together then pour into individual dishes. Chill well and serve with brandy snaps.

Note
Belinda Lang says this is excellent for anyone who isn't keen on making desserts or if there isn't enough time.

FRUIT BRÛLÉE

Recipe sent by
Lesley Joseph

Ingredients

Serves 4-6

1 tin lychees
1 tin mangoes
1 tin peaches
½ bunch grapes
1 large tub crème fraîche
brown sugar
mini macaroon or ratafia biscuits

Method

De-pip the grapes, cut in half and put in the bottom of an ovenproof
dish. Drain all the juice from the tinned fruits and lay the fruits in the
dish with the grapes. Crunch up the ratafia biscuits and sprinkle on top
of the fruits. Spread the crème fraîche on top of the biscuits and fruit
mixture and smooth evenly to the edges. Sprinkle the sugar on top and
pop under a hot grill until the sugar caramelises.

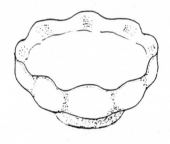

MARLBOROUGH TART

Recipe sent by
Moray Watson

Ingredients

Serves 4-6

175/225 g (6 - 8 oz) puff pastry
75 g (3 oz) mixed peel
6 glacé cherries
175 g (6 oz) butter
175 g (6 oz) demerara sugar
4 egg yolks
½ lemon

Method

Roll out the pastry and line a flan tin with it. Chop the mixed peel and cherries finely and sprinkle evenly over the pastry. Mix the butter and sugar in a pan over a low heat until melted, add the egg yolks and the grated rind and a squeeze of the lemon and cook for 1 minute. Then pour the mixture into the pastry case. Bake in a medium oven for ½ hour until set and the pastry cooked.

Note

This is a great favourite with the Moray Watson family. Moray says they found it 30 years ago in Scotland. It can be eaten hot or cold.

FRESH LEMON CHEESECAKE WITH FROSTED GRAPES

Recipe sent by
Gaynor Fraser

Ingredients

Serves 6-8

For the filling
350 g (12 oz) cottage cheese
10 g (½ oz) powdered gelatine
2 large egg yolks
60 g (2½ oz) caster sugar
grated rind and juice of 2 lemons
150 ml (5 fl oz) double cream

For the base
110 g (4 oz) digestive biscuits
50 g (2 oz) butter

For the topping
1 egg white
110 g (4 oz) seedless grapes
caster sugar

Method

Lightly oil an 8 inch (20 cm) flan tin or sponge tin with a loose base. First prepare the base by melting the butter in a small saucepan, then mix the melted butter with the biscuit crumbs in a bowl. Spoon the mixture into the prepared tin and press down well all over as evenly as possible. Put the gelatine along with 3 tablespoons of cold water into a small cup and stand this in a saucepan of barely simmering water. Leave for about 10 minutes until the gelatine looks clear and transparent. Then put on one side. Now put the egg yolks, sugar and cheese in a liquidiser, blend for 1 minute, then add the lemon juice and rind plus the gelatine (pour the gelatine through a strainer). Blend again until everything is smooth. Now whip up the cream until you get a floppy consistency, pour this into the liquidiser and blend again for a few seconds. Next pour this over the base, cover with foil and chill for a minimum of 3 hours.

Meanwhile whisk the egg white. Break up the grapes into little clusters of two or three grapes and dip each bunch into the egg white, then in the saucer of caster sugar. Leave them spread out on greaseproof paper for a couple of hours before using them for decoration.

Note

Gaynor writes "Sophie and I became close friends during a run of 'The Scarlet Pimpernel' at Her Majesty's in 1985 and we soon discovered that our tastes in nearly all things were very much alike, especially for the sweet things in life! Sophie prepared this delicious dessert for me at her home in Watford. After 'digs' and 'naff caffs' on tour, real food in a real home was sheer bliss. The frosted grapes were that final touch of luxury." Copyright Delia Smith 1987. Recipe reproduced by permission from Delia Smith's *Complete Illustrated Cookery Course* published by BBC Books.

CROISSANTS CORDON BLEU

Recipe sent by
Patrick Anthony

Ingredients   Serves 4-6

115 g (4 oz) dried apricots, chopped
2 tablespoons orange liqueur (Cointreau ideal)
6 croissants
55 g (2 oz) butter, melted
85- 115 g (3 - 4 oz) apricot preserve
300 ml (10 fl oz) double cream
300 ml (10 fl oz) full cream milk
3 large eggs plus 2 egg yolks
55 g (2 oz) caster sugar
½ vanilla pod or 1 teaspoon essence
icing sugar and pouring cream to serve

Method

Preheat the oven to 170°C (325°F) gas mark 3. Steep the apricots in the orange liqueur. Butter a large, deep dish with unsalted butter. Split the croissants in half, brush the cut sides with melted butter and spread with apricot preserve, then reassemble in sandwich fashion. Sprinkle the base of the dish with the soaked apricot pieces and place the croissants on top then prick them with a sharp carving fork. In a bowl beat the eggs and yolks with the sugar. In a saucepan gently bring the cream, milk and vanilla to the boil, remove the vanilla pod and slowly pour the hot mixture over the eggs, whisking continuously. Ladle the custard over the croissants. Place the dish inside a larger tin and pour in sufficient hot water to come halfway up the sides. (This water bath will protect the custard from burning.) Cover with foil and bake for 35 minutes then remove the foil and bake for 10 more minutes or until the custard is set. Dredge with icing sugar accompanied by cream. Serve hot or cold.

Note

Patrick was food filming in Paris and having done a street market, The Brasserie, La Cupole, Pollaine the Breadmaker, Fauchon the grocer AND a specialist cheese shop, it was his task to demonstrate at the Cordon Bleu School in front of international mature students. His desire to fly the British flag resulted in this luxury bread and butter pudding theme, employing the croissant as a gesture to his hosts.

BREAD AND BUTTER PUDDING

Recipe sent by
Dame Judi Dench

Ingredients   Serves 4

275 ml (½ pint) milk
70 ml double cream
grated rind of half a small lemon
50 g (2 oz) caster sugar
3 eggs
Pannetone cake
10 g (½ oz candied lemon or orange peel, finely chopped
50 g (2 oz) currants
freshly grated nutmeg

Method

Heat the oven to 180°C (350°F) gas mark 4. Butter a 1 litre (2 pint) oblong baking dish. Slice the Pannetone and butter it. Put one layer on the base of the dish, sprinkle with the candied peel and half the currants. Put another layer of Pannetone in the dish and sprinkle with the rest of the currants. Put the milk and cream together in a measuring jug, stir in the lemon peel and sugar. Whisk the eggs in a small basin and add to the milk mixture. Pour the whole lot over the Pannetone and sprinkle with the nutmeg. Bake for 30-40 minutes until lightly set. Serve warm.

Note

'This is delicious and provides the perfect solution for what to do with those dry Italian cakes you get given at Christmas', says Dame Judi.

TIPSY RING

Recipe sent by
Desmond Barrit

Ingredients   Serves 6-8

2 packets biscuits (gingernuts are great)
1 cup alcohol (brandy, sherry, cointreau or whatever you like)
570 ml (1 pint) double cream
sprinkling of drinking chocolate

Method

Whip the cream to peaks. Dunk each biscuit briefly into the alcohol. Dab a teaspoon of cream onto one side. Dunk another biscuit and sandwich it onto the cream. Dab on another spoonful of cream and repeat and repeat! Eventually you will end up with a ring of biscuits sandwiched with cream and dunked in alcohol. Cover the ring with the remaining cream and put it in the fridge for at least 2 hours. Before serving sieve a little drinking chocolate over the top.

Note

This is so rich it will probably serve up to 8 people. Orange juice can be used instead of alcohol. Enjoy!

STINK - PUFF

**Recipe sent by
Christopher Timothy**

Ingredients   Serves 6
1 packet of strawberry or raspberry jelly
1 can carnation milk

Method
Dissolve the jelly cubes with less than the recommendation on the
packet. Whisking the while, add the carnation milk, pouring slowly.
Continue to whisk until the mixture is thick, evenly coloured and
creamy. This of course can be achieved with the use of a blender,
electric mixer, etc but whisking is the way my Mother used to do it and
what's good enough for my Mother ... etc! Leave to set in a cool place
and chill before serving.

Note
It's thick, creamy, calorie-ridden and probably a tad too sweet and
DELICIOUS!

Stink-puff is an anagram.

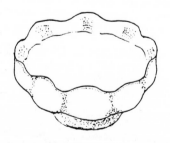

PERE AL FORNO
Baked Pears

Recipe sent by
Robert Demeger

Ingredients
1 large pear per person
50 ml (2 oz) caster sugar
200 ml (2 fl oz) dry Marsala
cinnamon stick
vanilla pod
100 ml (3 fl oz) water

Method
Stand the pears, unpeeled, in a high-sided ovenproof dish. Add the
Marsala and water so that the liquid comes about halfway up the pears.
Add the sugar, cinnamon stick and vanilla pod. Bake uncovered for 1½ -
2 hours at 150°C (300°F) gas mark 2. They can be served hot or cold,
with the juice poured over the pears. Cream or mascarpone can be
added if desired.

Note
'This is a delicious dessert which should be better known - it makes a
welcome change from pears in red wine', says Robert Demeger.

REDCURRANT AND RASPBERRY ICE CREAM

**Recipe sent by
Rita Morrison
Serves 4**

Ingredients
340 g (¾ lb) raspberries
115 g (4 oz) redcurrants
140 g (5 oz) caster sugar
75 ml (⅛ pint) water
140 ml (¼ pint) double cream

Method
Purée the raspberries and redcurrants and press through a sieve. Boil the sugar and water gently together for 3 minutes. Leave to cool, then stir the syrup into the fruit purée. Now fold in the lightly whipped double cream and spoon into a polythene freezer box. Freeze in the icebox of the fridge or freezer for between 2-3 hours until half frozen. At this stage beat the mixture with a hand whisk, then freeze until needed. To serve, decorate with sprigs of mint and a 'necklace' of frosted redcurrants by rolling the berries in caster sugar and then freezing for approximately 30 minutes.

Note
When Rita lived in Scarborough, the finest vanilla ice cream in the world was found at the Harbour Bar Ice-Cream Parlour on the sea-front, but in July, when the redcurrant bushes were laden with clusters of rich red tangy jewels, she combined the two berries to make this ice cream with a flavour of pure summer.

INFALLIBLE ICE CREAM

**Recipe sent by
Juliet Stevenson**

Ingredients   Serves 4
450 g (1 lb) frozen berries (raspberries, strawberries, blackberries)
2 tablespoons water
225 g (½ lb) icing sugar
275 ml (½ pint) whipping cream
juice of ½ lemon

Method
Put the fruit into a pan with the water. Cover and simmer very gently
for 8-10 minutes till tender. Leave to cool. Sieve or mouli to remove
pips and skin. Add icing sugar and lemon juice. Whip the cream till it
hangs on the whisk. Fold into the cold purée. Turn into a container
and leave in the freezer for 1 hour or until frozen for 1 inch round the
edge. Turn into a bowl and beat with whisk or fork till smooth and
creamy. Return to freezer until needed.

Note
This is Juliet Stevenson's mother-in-law's ice cream recipe: a fool-proof
recipe for Häagen-Dazs lovers who can't afford it all the time!

MARY GRIFFITHS' 'RECEIPT' FOR POTATO FLOUR CHOCOLATE CAKE
(Invaluable for non wheat eaters)

Recipe sent by
Ann Penfold

Ingredients

125 g (5 oz) butter

50 g (2 oz) potato flour

3 eggs

125 g (5 oz) good plain chocolate

½ teaspoon baking powder

100 g (4 oz) castor sugar

Method

Grease a cake tin. Preheat the oven to 150°C (300°F) gas mark 3. Melt the butter and chocolate in a large pan. Then add the potato flour and baking powder. Separate 3 eggs and beat the yolks with the sugar. Add to the melted chocolate mixture. Beat the whites until stiff in a large bowl. Add everything in the pan to the whites and fold together. Pour into the greased tin and bake until set. Test with a skewer which should come out clean.

Note

'An abiding memory of Sophie is our helpless laughter as she growled at the Green Room fridge in Scarborough knowing something delicious was inside for the company tea', says Ann Penfold. This recipe was given to Ann in the early seventies by a wonderful actress called Mary Griffiths. 'We were in the National Theatre production of 'Saturday, Sunday, Monday' at the Queen's Theatre, Shaftesbury Avenue and matinée days were cake-eating days. Sophie would have growled a lot!'

ALGARS

**Recipe sent by
Niamh Cusack**

Ingredients
110 g (4 oz) margarine or butter
110 g (4 oz) sugar (brown is nice or demerera)
a splash of vanilla essence
150 g (5 oz) plain flour
2 tablespoons cocoa
50 g (2 oz) crushed cornflakes

Method
Set the oven to 180°C (350°F) gas mark 4 and grease two baking trays. Beat the sugar, butter and vanilla until soft. Then add the flour, cocoa and cornflakes. Form the mixture into balls (walnut size) and press gently onto the greased trays with a space around each one. Bake for 8-10 minutes. They should retain a rounded shape. When cool put a dollop of melted chocolate on each biscuit.

Note
These biscuits are favourites of Niamh's family and she makes them with her young son Celene.

CHOCOLATE NUT CAKE

Recipe sent by Patricia Hodge

Ingredients
225 g (8 oz) margarine
225 g (8 oz) icing sugar
4 eggs
1½ teaspoons cinnamon
75 g (3 oz) grated chocolate
225 g (8 oz) ground almonds
Icing
75 g (3 oz) plain chocolate
110 g (4 oz) icing sugar
1½ teaspoons nut oil

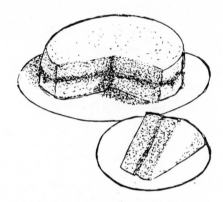

Method
Cream the margarine and sugar. Beat in the eggs alternately with the chocolate and almonds. Bake in a 23 cm (9 inch) farm tin for about 45 minutes at 180°C (350°F) gas mark 4. Leave to cool in the tin. Melt the chocolate in a saucepan and stir in the nut oil and sugar and a little water if it is too stiff. Spread over the cake and leave 48 hours before cutting.

Note
According to Patricia Hodge this is a truly delicious, not to say fattening recipe and one she would recommend to anyone the day after they come off their diet!

BROWN SODA BREAD

**Recipe sent by
Claire Skinner**

Ingredients
450 g (1 lb) brown stone ground flour
175 g (6 oz) white flour
2.5 ml (½ teaspoon) baking soda
2.5 ml (½ teaspoon) salt
50 g (2 oz) butter (optional)
buttermilk or soured cream
1 small egg

Method
Mix all the dry ingredients together. If using butter mix it in with your
fingertips. Work in the buttermilk and egg. The mixture must be really
wet so that it only just holds its shape. Place on a greased, floured
baking tray and shake it to settle it flat. Cut a deep cross firmly into the
top. Bake at 200°C (400°F) gas mark 6 for 40 minutes until firm and
browned.

Note
This is a very simple recipe which reminds Claire Skinner of a holiday
staying with her auntie in Ireland, who had to make loaf after loaf to
keep up with Claire's consumption. Claire has now started to make it
for herself. The recipe is from Elizabeth Luard's *'Country Cooking'*
published by Ebury Press.

WALNUT AND APRICOT BREAD

Recipe sent by
Nick Nairn

Ingredients

25 g (1 oz) fresh yeast
600 ml (20 fl oz) warm water
50 ml (2 fl oz) olive oil
1 kg (2 lb) strong plain flour

50 ml (2 fl oz) walnut oil
25 g (1 oz) salt
125 g (4½ oz) walnuts
75 g (3 oz) diced dried apricots

Method

Preheat the oven to 230°C (450°F) gas mark 8. Dissolve the yeast in the water and place in a mixing bowl. Add the oil and flour and bring together to form a dough. Remove from the bowl and knead it for seven minutes. Add the walnuts and apricots and work for a further three minutes. Cut the dough into six pieces and roll into sausage shapes about 12 cm (5 inches) long and 5 cm (2 inches) wide. Place on a floured baking sheet, cover with a damp baking towel and leave to prove for about 30 minutes in a warm place until doubled in size. Don't worry if the rolls join together. Place a tray half-filled with water in the bottom of the oven and leave for 10 minutes to produce steam to make the oven moist which will help the bread to rise and give it a nice crisp crust. Place the loaves in the middle of the oven for 25 - 30 minutes. They should be golden brown on top when ready and sound hollow when tapped on the bottom. Remove and leave on a rack to cool. Dust each one with flour and eat immediately or wrap individually in clingfilm and freeze. This makes 6 medium loaves.

Note

Nick says that after a visit to the theatre he loves this bread toasted with cheese and ham or lots of unsalted butter. The flavour of the apricots and walnuts goes well with a creamy blue cheese such as Dunsyre Blue. A really special bread makes a really special supper.